Praise for *Empowering Public Wisdom*

"At last someone has described the conditions under which ordinary people can generate real public wisdom. The implications for democracy—especially for democratic handling of our most troubling, complex, and urgent issues—are profound. I urge activists, academics, public officials, and every concerned citizen to heed the call in this book."—Richard Sclove, author of *Democracy and Technology*

"*Empowering Public Wisdom* serves up a juicy antidote to today's increasingly intractable issues, political gridlock, and public disengagement. Having used many of the practices Atlee outlines, I can attest to the viability and vitality of the vision he paints and the approaches he proposes on behalf of us all."—Peggy Holman, consultant, author of *Engaging Emergence: Turning Upheaval into Opportunity* and coauthor of *The Change Handbook*

"In this book, Tom Atlee highlights the seldom-noted potential of dialogue and deliberation to generate true public wisdom. He explores how to increase that potential, how to embed it in our democracy, and how to empower it to make a real difference—an important contribution to our field and our political culture."—Sandy Heierbacher, director, National Coalition for Dialogue & Deliberation

Empowering Public Wisdom

A Practical Vision of Citizen-Led Politics

Tom Atlee

Berkeley, California

Published by Evolver Editions,
an imprint of North Atlantic Books
P.O. Box 12327
Berkeley, California 94712

Cover art and photography © EDHAR/Shutterstock.com and
    maxstockphoto/Shutterstock.com
Art direction and design by michaelrobinsonnyc.com
Book design by Brad Greene
Printed in the United States of America

Empowering Public Wisdom: A Practical Vision of Citizen-Led Politics
is sponsored by the Society for the Study of Native Arts and Sciences, a nonprofit educational corporation whose goals are to
develop an educational and cross-cultural perspective linking
various scientific, social, and artistic fields; to nurture a holistic
view of arts, sciences, humanities, and healing; and to publish and
distribute literature on the relationship of mind, body, and nature.

North Atlantic Books' publications are available through
most bookstores. For further information, visit our website
at www.northatlanticbooks.com or call 800-733-3000.

Library of Congress Cataloging-in-Publication Data

Atlee, Tom, 1947–
  Empowering public wisdom: a practical vision of citizen-led poli-
tics/Tom Atlee.
      p. cm.
  ISBN 978-1-58394-500-1
  1. Direct democracy. 2. Deliberative democracy. 3. Political participation. 4. Political planning—Citizen participation. 5. Decision
making—Citizen participation. I. Title.
  JC423.A82 2012
  321.8—dc23

                                                        2012004365

1 2 3 4 5 6 7 8 9 UNITED 17 16 15 14 13 12
Printed on recycled paper

The deliberative sense of the community should govern.

— Alexander Hamilton

The foundation of democracy is faith in ... human intelligence and in the power of pooled and cooperative experience ... to generate progressively the knowledge and wisdom needed to guide collective action.

—John Dewey

To all who carry the dream
of collective wisdom
in all its forms

～

Acknowledgments

I wish to thank some colleagues in this journey, who had tremendous impact on my sense of possibilities—including Jim Rough, Ned Crosby, George Por, Dick Sclove, Janette Hartz-Karp, Peggy Holman, Kaliya Hamlin, Juanita Brown, Rosa Zubizarreta, Sandy Heierbacher, Joseph McCormick, Steve Bhaerman, Kenoli Oleari, Eileen Palmer, Tree Bressen, Steven Kull, Frances Moore Lappé, Eryn Kalish, Jeff Golden, Sen. Les Ihara, Nancy Bordier, Jean-François Noubel, John Gastil, Jeff Groethe, Charles M. Johnston, Helene Landemore, and Fran Peavey.

I want to thank Michael Dowd and Connie Barlow for drawing me into the sacred evolutionary Great Story that contains and makes so much useful meaning of my current efforts—and Peter Senge, Marshall Rosenberg, Margaret Wheatley, Rob Hopkins, Bill Mollison, Charles Eisenstein, David Bohm, Arny Mindell, Donella Meadows, Howard Gardner, and Christopher Alexander for pioneering new memes that profoundly influenced my work.

I also wish to thank the many board members and supporters of the Co-Intelligence Institute, who made—and make—it possible for me to continue my research, networking, and visionary work—especially Adin Rogovin, John Abbe, Heather Tischbein, Lyn Bazzell, Kevin Reidy, Miki Kashtan, Elliot Shuford, Lynne Swift, Carolyn Shaffer, Elizabeth York, Diana Morley, Mary Ann Gallagher, Grant Abert, John Steiner, Michelle Mercer,

Lysa Leland, Bruce Nayowith, Anne Henny, Christian Forthomme, Laura Loescher, Jean Houston, Jeannine Laprad, Pat Benn, and Stephen Silha—and my treasured friends and colleagues, Peter Chabarek, Susan Cannon, Robert Steele, Sheri Herndon, Ben Roberts, Matt McRae, and Sarah Shmigelsky.

I am grateful for the support of my publisher, Doug Reil, and my wonderful editor, Erin Wiegand, whose collaborative spirit, respect, and insightful understanding of the underlying vision of this book made working with her a true delight.

Finally, I want to think my family—my parents, John and Elinore; my brother, Dick; my daughter, Jennifer; my late life partner, Karen Mercer; and my current life partner, Dulcy Lee—for their remarkable love and support.

Tom Atlee
Eugene, Oregon
May 3, 2012

Contents

APPENDICES

Preface

In March 1986, the cross-country Great Peace March, which had launched two weeks earlier from Los Angeles with 1,200 people, went bankrupt and was thrown into chaos in the Mojave Desert. About 800 marchers and almost all the paid staff left. Most of the support vehicles were repossessed. With no formal leadership or resources, the 400 remaining marchers—myself included—camped out for two weeks in a BMX track in Barstow, arguing and talking in circles, trying to figure out what to do next.

Nine months later—quite remarkably—the March arrived in Washington DC with 1,200 people, after self-organizing its way—fifteen to twenty-five miles a day in every kind of weather—all the way across the continent. That's where I first learned about self-organization, collective intelligence, and collective wisdom.

My concerns about the fate of the planet have remained keen my entire life. Born into the threat of nuclear holocaust, I came of age during the Vietnam War. I matured during growing environmental catastrophes, critical resource depletion, and corroding civil liberties. In the last few years, I have become an elder in the midst of economic collapse, social unrest, and increasing climate chaos.

Most of these issues and many others are extremely urgent. Nevertheless, I have become less of an issue-oriented activist as I have grown older. It has become quite clear to me that most of our issues and crises come from the way we have things set up—our social, political, and economic systems—and from the stories we tell ourselves about who we are and what we're doing here. Starting in the late 1980s I began to see that what we needed was not so much solutions to our problems as a deep transformation of our faulty systems and stories. After all, I had learned from my experience on the Great Peace March that a healthy living system can and will solve its own problems if it can just organize itself in a way that allows that.

So if that is the case, I wondered, where should I put my energy and attention as a change agent?

For years after the Great Peace March I became fascinated with *intelligence* as the dynamic capacity we use to align our ideas, stories, and models of the world with the way the world actually is. We make a mental map of reality and then take actions based on that map. When our actions succeed, that suggests our map is a good one. When we mess up, that means our map was wrong in some way. Then, to the extent we're intelligent, we revise our map and try again. This, of course, is what learning is all about.

I realized that when a society persists in messing up the world it depends on and continues to create more powerful means to destroy itself, it is not only operating on faulty maps of itself and its world but lacks adequate means to correct those maps. In some important way, it lacks intelligence—collective intelligence—and so keeps on doing collectively stupid, unwise things.

I soon realized that lack of collective intelligence is not related to the intelligence of the society's individual members. It seems odd, but I learned that really smart people can generate a phenomenal amount of collective stupidity, simply by getting in each other's way or by having faulty data to work with.

At the same time, I realized that our society has an awesome amount of collective intelligence already. Look at science and the ever-evolving mass of cocreated knowledge in libraries, educational institutions, and the internet. So what's going on here? How can society be collectively smart and stupid at the same time?

I narrowed my target.

I realized two facts: first, different sectors of our society have different amounts and kinds of collective intelligence that don't always fit together. For example, the collective intelligence of medical science collides with the collective intelligence of millions of people using alternative healing practices, and both of those groups collide with the collective intelligence of the bean counters in health insurance companies.

Second, I saw that intelligence is often applied successfully but very narrowly, creating problems in the areas that weren't adequately taken into account. We reduce unemployment by hiring people to build more weapons, but end up with wars and skyrocketing debt. We build amazing highway systems to facilitate traffic and end up with unsustainable suburbs and chaotic weather.

We can easily see both of these dynamics—the diverse quality of collective intelligence and its narrow applications—playing out in our politics and governance today.

The collective intelligence of science tells us what's going on with climate change. But that scientific knowledge may have little impact on our public policies. Something breaks down between what "we" know and what "we" do.

Part of the problem is that there is no coherent "we"— no embodiment of the whole society—that is taking in the knowledge and applying it to policy. The left hand doesn't know (or often care) what the right hand is doing. Another part of the problem is that our policymakers focus on getting reelected every two to six years by majority vote. Most voters focus on short-term self-interest and/or mental models that are continually manipulated by special interests. These narrow focuses then play out in a political culture based on partisan battle instead of collective learning and collaboration. Is it any surprise that long-term inclusive wisdom is not what we get from our decision-making systems?

It became clear that I needed to move beyond general theories of collective intelligence to focus on how our democratic decision-making systems can routinely generate citizen-based collective wisdom that has real impact. I call that ideal *empowered public wisdom.*

Over the last two decades I've learned a lot about where wisdom comes from and how it can be generated by ordinary people so they can use it to govern their collective affairs. In this book I share what I've found, including proven methods, leading-edge research, and thrilling visions of what is possible now.

Since virtually every issue has to make its way through our political and governance systems before it is addressed by the society as a whole—and because those systems are currently incapable of dealing with those issues wisely, and because our foolish, dangerous policies now threaten the very survival of civilization and life on earth—I basically let go of all the other issues I was concerned about in order to focus on this.

I urge you to do the same.

Manifesto:
A Call to Establish a Legitimate, Wise, Inclusive, and Powerful Collective Voice of the People

We are in serious trouble. And we face epoch-making opportunities to remake our world in the face of that trouble in profoundly positive ways.

As unprecedented crises emerge, our democratic republic—the tool we use to deal with *all* our public issues—is breaking down. We urgently need new approaches that can make us wise masters of our own common destiny. Luckily, the resources for wise self-governance and ongoing cocreativity are at our fingertips.

Even as we increase the diversity, power, and connectivity of our *individual voices,* it is becoming possible for We the People, as a whole, to speak with *one wise voice:*

- a voice that only speaks after considering all sides of each issue and viewing its full complexity;
- a voice that embraces the diverse perspectives, values, stories, needs, and dreams of the entire community, state, or country for which it speaks;
- a voice that takes into consideration the big picture, the long term, and what could happen, both good and bad; and
- a voice that is respected by the vast majority of the population as our legitimate collective voice.

We can and must create that voice in our democracy now. And we can and must give it a powerful role in deciding what will happen. Our lives, our communities, our country, our world, and our collective future depend on it.

Why a Wise Public Voice Is Essential

In a world where our collective problems are becoming catastrophic, we find our collective destiny in the hands of competing interests that seldom serve our shared well-being or address the true complexity of our public issues. Their partial, partisan, and temporary solutions all too often make our problems worse. When we hear someone speak for the common good, he or she is easily marginalized as just one more special interest.

Yet *real* special interests are continuously manipulating us using scientific public relations, media, and mountains of money. We have little opportunity or time to deliberate together, to explore our differences and our common interests, or to develop and express our united public judgment and community wisdom on issues that impact our lives. We are kept busy and entertained, divided and conquered.

Until We the People create a coherent, wise, collective voice, our interests will not be served and no public issue will be handled wisely.

Why a Wise Public Voice Is Possible

Methods abound to translate differences and conflicts into greater insight and cocreativity. And ways exist to provide full-spectrum information and use it to generate collective understanding. Under the right conditions, wise public decisions can be produced by facilitating deliberations among a relatively small group of ordinary citizens whose diversity makes them a microcosm of the community from which they were drawn. Few people realize that hundreds of such *citizen deliberative councils* have been held successfully all over the world.

By broadly advocating, developing, using, and institutionalizing such councils we can generate a legitimate, wise, inclusive, coherent, and powerful voice of the people—an authentic voice of the whole public.

Why Nothing Else Can Really Serve That Purpose

Public opinion polls tell how many of us believe this or that off the top of our heads. They do not reflect what we would believe if we were fully informed and had considered each other's points of view productively. Pundits, politicians, and experts tell us what we should believe, but they seldom help us work toward a consensus that embraces our collective diversity and our shared needs and aspirations. Talk shows, public hearings, and protests are filled with people passionate about their perspectives, but they seldom actually *hear* each other or work to find the common ground needed to move ahead as whole communities.

We now know how to bring the actual diversity of the public together to find a shared voice of community wisdom that makes sense for our whole community, our whole country. We just need to convene temporary citizen deliberative councils with a membership that embodies the diversity of their community or country. Have them deliberate for days or weeks about a specific public concern. Help them report their findings and recommendations to officials, the media, and the public—and then organize around those recommendations. Then watch how a powerful and shared understanding emerges about what needs to be done.

Citizen deliberative councils have proven successful with even the most technical, complex issues. They have been used to bring forth inspiring visions. They have been used to evaluate legislation and politicians and to provide those evaluations to the voters. Every time, we find that this authentic public voice speaks the language of neither the Left nor the Right. It simply reveals the best common sense of the community.

What makes these councils so special? Members are chosen at random or scientifically or both, so they can be convened as an accurate microcosm of the public—diverse, temporary, and hard to corrupt. They aren't ignorant; they're given full information about the issue they are considering. And they don't just argue, spouting opinions off the top of their heads; they talk, listen, learn, and think *together.* Like trial juries, they rise to the occasion and work hard to do a good job for their community or country. They succeed remarkably often and well.

Other approaches to public dialogue, deliberation, participation, and input are vital to a thriving democracy of engaged citizens. But most do not provide the information, time, and support needed to generate a valid, coherent, wise voice of the whole populace. They may engage and educate individual voters about the issues, but they don't tell us what a truly informed, thoughtful, and creatively interacting citizenry would decide together about specific government policies, laws, budgets, taxes, and programs.

Without a collective voice of the whole citizenry to speak wisely and powerfully in our public life, we have become impoverished and imperiled. We need to change that—soon.

Our children—and their children's children—need us to create this powerful collective voice, because it is their voice too. They need us to ensure that it is wise and heeded, because we and they urgently need our politics and our governance to become sensible, sustainable, creative, and just. Our times are perilous. Nearly everything we love is at stake.

Thomas Paine once said, in his revolutionary pamphlet *Common Sense,* "We have it in our power to begin the world again." It is so, even now.

We have it in our power to call forth a voice that speaks our best collective wisdom. We have it in our power to cease collectively degrading our lives and destroying our world. We have it in our power to create a new world together—a world that is a true joy for our children—and their children—to live in. We can and must create a voice that can speak this urgent truth for all of us.

And with that voice, we will begin the world again, and again, and again. . . .

PART ONE

A Wiser Democracy—
Taking It Seriously

CHAPTER 1

Democracy Is about Power— and the People

Democracy—all politics—is about power: who has it and how they use it. Do people try to dominate each other and the world? Do they work together for the common good? Do they have the freedom to develop and use their own personal and collective power?

If we want to preserve and expand democracy, we need to understand some important facts about power.

Power, Social Power, and Personal Power

Power is the ability to do, to act, to have an effect, to influence life. This is *power-to*, the most fundamental form of power: simply the power to accomplish things. Democracy is about the power that we, the people, have—the power to do the things that we, as individuals and collectively, want to do and that need doing.

Power-to involves freedom—freedom-from (freedom from barriers, oppression, and harm) and freedom-to (freedom to take effective action). Freedom-from is what most people think of when they think of freedom. But there's this other freedom, as well: freedom-to. We don't really have freedom to do, be, or have something unless we have both opportunity and possibility to achieve it. Most of us are not, realistically speaking, free to suspend ourselves in midair (except in outer space). Someone who has no legs is not, realistically speaking, free to walk up ten flights of stairs.

So democracy is partly about keeping our commons—the shared life-spaces where we all live together—both unhampered by unreasonable limits (freedom-from) and rich with equal opportunities (freedom-to). We want to be able to speak out, get together, enter buildings in wheelchairs, be fairly considered for jobs, and all the rest. Democracy doesn't always or necessarily mean we will be helped—although we might be, if that is the will of our fellows—but it does mean that we should have rights and opportunities comparable to everyone else's. How we use those rights and opportunities is up to us—as long as we don't undermine other people's rights and freedoms in the process.

The fact that our freedom exists in the context of other people's freedom means that freedom can never be absolute. But it can be optimized: that is, it can be made as broad and full as possible for everyone involved, given the limitations of the circumstances. Working that out is—or should be—one of the great ongoing projects of our democratic life. It helps a lot if we respect and listen to each other. It makes a difference if we then use what we learn to search together for good answers that benefit us all.

Freedom and power are linked at the hip. You will never find one without the other.

Which brings us back to power. Power-to breaks down into a number of other types of power. The form of power most people think of is *power-over*. Power-over is the ability to control, determine, dominate, or destroy—or unduly influence—someone or something. We apply power-over in many parts of our individual and collective lives, from controlling cars and hammers to building and bombing skyscrapers to managing amber waves of grain and kids at the dinner table.

When power-over translates into social power, it means the ability to control society, to dominate opponents, to garner greater privileges, to win in political and economic battlegrounds. People and groups with superior weapons, knowledge of scientific public relations, tons of money, authority to imprison people, and/or ownership of mass media have an abundance of power-over. Even individual qualities like intelligence, creativity, sexuality, and personality can provide power-over in social situations.

Ideally, in a democracy, social power (of the power-over variety) is distributed broadly, fairly, and relatively evenly, so that it doesn't distort our ability to make good public decisions and treat each other decently. This helps us ensure an appropriate level of freedom for all concerned. Decentralization, human rights, and social justice and equity are all democratic principles that support the distribution of social power.

However, there is often need for social power to be centralized or concentrated. Some functions are naturally best handled at a particular level of society—personal, local, state, national, international. Ideally a function would be assigned to the lowest level at which it can be effectively handled. For example, most people believe that a country's defense is best addressed at the national level, rather than at the county or individual citizen levels. Obviously, care for the oceans needs to be done at transnational, even global levels. On the other hand, the structure of your ongoing education is best left to you, personally, although local school boards and state and national legislatures may deem it appropriate to have certain broadly applied standards for a diploma or certificate that is recognized by the whole society.

When social power is centralized or concentrated it poses a *potential* threat to democracy. As Lord Acton famously said: "Power tends to corrupt and absolute power corrupts absolutely." Two strategies help make concentrated power more benign. One is to *balance* it with other centers of concentrated social power. For example, the three branches of the U.S. government—legislative, administrative, and judicial—were designed to "check and balance" each other. Each branch has certain specified powers, but can be challenged, bypassed, or overruled by the other branches in specific ways and circumstances. Unions and corporate leaders have powers that balance each other, at least somewhat. Lately we've seen small groups and movements—from terrorists to nonviolent activists like Martin Luther King, Jr., from Occupy Wall Street to hackers and bloggers—balance the concentrated power of giant national and transnational institutions, at least somewhat. In a healthy democracy, whenever power gets too concentrated, other powers show up to challenge and attempt to balance it.

The second strategy to make concentrated power more benign is to make it *answerable* to those over whom it is exercised. This is why government transparency, investigative journalism, whistleblowers, and civilian oversight of police, military, and intelligence services are so important. Elections also constitute a powerful form of answerability, if they are fair and done in a context where we, the people, actually know what public officials have been doing and who is funding their electoral campaigns. The answerability principle is also why corporations—some of which are arguably the best examples of concentrated power on earth today—are supposed to be chartered by the community or state, and their performance reviewed before the charter is periodically renewed or withdrawn.

If a group, organization, or person with undue concentrated power resists all efforts to balance their power or make it answerable, that power needs be broken up and/or its functions distributed to others. This is usually quite difficult, but we've seen examples ranging from antitrust laws to the American Revolution.

One way or another, if we wish to preserve our democracy we must mitigate the toxic tendencies of concentrated power.

However—and this is a key point—all these safeguards are only necessary because we're talking about power-over. There's another form of power—*power-with,* the power of collaboration and synergy—which is equally valuable whether it is distributed or concentrated. Working together—especially when we use our differences well—makes each of us more powerful. All of us together know more and can do more than any of us individually. Working together we can usually serve our self-interest better than if we fight for what we want against the self-interest of others.

At any given time in the development of a group or culture, there will be things that people can agree on and things they can't agree on. Power-with is clearly the best choice for achieving what we agree on. Power-over is clearly workable—in a sort of rough-and-tumble way—for those things we can't agree on: either someone with dominant power tells everyone else what to do, or there's a contest to see who can win enough power to make the others comply or back down—the idea behind majority voting.

What's interesting about what's going on in our society right now is that power-with strategies—especially quality conversation—are increasingly being used to expand the territory of what we can agree on. This is true even though we're seeing more polarized battles and power plays in politics, economics, and many other spheres.

Key developments in the recent popularity of power-with strategies include Roger Fisher and William Ury's watershed 1981 book, *Getting to Yes,* in which they explain "Principled Negotiation." They encourage adversarial negotiators to stop fighting, manipulating, and compromising, and instead work together to identify the legitimate interests of all sides and then work together to figure out how to satisfy those legitimate interests.

Marshall Rosenberg's Nonviolent Communication practice provides a way to dig below people's disagreeable behaviors to the emotions that drive those behaviors, and then to dig further to understand the unmet basic needs that evoke those emotions, and finally to look together for strategies that will satisfy those basic needs in ways that are agreeable to everyone involved.

Future Search conferences bring key players involved in a situation together to review their shared (and usually problematic) past, to look together at shared current realities, and to "search for common ground"—that is, visions they all can buy into and projects they can work on together. Differences get noted and set aside while participants focus on the search for common ground.

The prominent international nonprofit Search for Common Ground works in two dozen conflicted countries getting adversaries to hear each other's views; identify common fears, hopes, and interests; and work to develop solutions that address as many of their interests as possible.

In the last decade even more potent methods like Dynamic Facilitation have been developed that use the energy and information-rich substance of conflict itself to come to collective breakthroughs and unprecedented *ah-ha!* solutions. It turns out that when people feel fully and authentically heard, as they are in Dynamic Facilitation, they stop pushing and resisting and begin to start listening to each other. When most everyone in the group has been well heard—and all participants become more clearly aware of the full complexity of their situation—they find themselves working together to address the "mess" of the whole situation. Often they end up going deeper or wider, or jumping totally "out of the box"; they understand the problem in new ways; and they arrive at unexpectedly creative solutions.

These examples are just the tip of the iceberg of what we already can do to address differences and conflicts—*if we want to and if we know how.* These and other methods will be explored further in this book.

Although such methods don't always work for all people in all situations, the number of people and situations for which they *do* work is increasing as the understanding and competence of theorists and practitioners grow. Power-with is fast becoming as strategic and skilled a science as power-over. Even military and business schools are teaching the power of cooperation. Power-with is also becoming a source of power in sustainability practices—working *with* bugs and bacteria to compost garbage and recycle wastes or working *with* wind and water to generate energy. All fields and practices that stress collaboration are exercising power-with.

Feeding into this new capacity is our growing understanding of a third form of power: *power-from-within.* It starts with understanding the power available from people's passions, interests, and natural inclinations. Kids who are interested in a subject learn it with no one forcing them to. So-called Open Space conferences are set up to have no prior agendas, but rather to help people who share particular passions find each other, talk, and work together. Permaculture practitioners arrange plants, animals, and physical aspects of a garden site together so that every organism pursuing its own self-interest causes the whole designed ecosystem to readily yield benefits for every organism involved, including its human gardeners.

Power-from-within includes not only our passions but our special capacities. Every one of us has skills and talents, knowledge and experience, many forms of intelligence and spirit, perhaps even conscious connection to powers greater than ourselves. All these personal qualities contribute to our ability to shape what happens the world, as long as we appreciate, nurture, and use them. And all of them can be enhanced in groups and cultures that respect and encourage them in their members. Furthermore, groups themselves have collective capacities—including collective experience, intelligence, and resources greater than the sum of the individual members—they can tap as power-from-within.

So there is power in tapping the natural life energies, experience, and capacities that already exist in individuals and groups, in organizations and communities, in societies and the world. Many group process experts speak of "the magic in the middle"—which means that there is power and wisdom that arises from *within* and *among* the group's members. This power and wisdom does not come from the individuals themselves so much as from their interactions, from a kind of group energy or intelligence that shows up because these people are together. Their very presence together calls forth certain ideas or behaviors that would not have emerged otherwise—*if* their culture and interactions support that happening. Many transformational consultants claim that every living system—every person, community, and organization—has within it the answers it needs.

But this often depends on certain processes and ways of being together that build synergy between the life of the group and the individual lives of its members. The group enhances the individuals' thinking, feeling, and competence, and the individuals enhance the functionality and creativity of the group. Everyone involved—especially the facilitator or coach—works to enhance both of these dynamics.

This kind of group synergy is often dramatically demonstrated in sports teams and jazz ensembles who are "in the groove." Power-with and power-from-within merge into an almost aesthetic surge of power-to. This "group flow" is quite exciting to watch and even more thrilling to be part of. People "lose themselves" in the group—not by becoming smaller or less themselves, but by expanding to embrace more of the group's interactive power within their own capacities and responses. The distinction between self and group becomes meaningless because they are both subsumed in this higher form of power and intelligence that is thoroughly dependent on all of them and their in-tune interactions.

This synergy between power-with and power-from-within is not always as dramatic as what I've articulated here. But usually those involved feel it as an expansion of themselves, their awareness, and their role in the world. They have been empowered.

The fact that this can happen in groups working on public issues has profound significance for what we normally think of as "politics."

One of the things it means is that a group of separate citizens who come together in this way can find themselves expanding into a shared identity often experienced as *We the People*—a palpable sense of collective agency that is mythically in charge in a democracy. These folks know they have what's needed to make politics and government work. They know they were just ordinary citizens hours or days before, but now they've seen a new level of citizenship and a new level of power, freedom, and responsibility. They can *feel* how this *We the People* identity is a force to be reckoned with.

Who Is "The People" or "The Public"?

The dictionary defines *the people* as "the citizens of a country, especially when considered in relation to those who govern them." And it defines *the public* as "ordinary people in general; the community." In a democracy—theoretically, at least—the people govern themselves, and we speak of "public opinion" and "public will." So in this book, when I speak of either the people or the public—and especially when I use the phrase *We the People*—I am referring to the whole democratic citizenry—the inclusive community of civic persons—as the collective sovereign ruler of its society.

In the vision in this book, the public is not just a bunch of isolated disengaged individuals. It is *the people* in the sense of Lincoln's memorable phrase "a government of the people, by the people, for the people." *The public* or *the people* is a collective entity capable of exercising coherent political agency on its own behalf. It is the sovereign in a self-governing society. It is the entity that created the U.S. Constitution—and this *people* can show up as sovereign at any time and place that "it" chooses to. In this book, the public—We the People—is whose voice we are looking for—comparable to the voice we hear in public opinion polls, but more coherent and wise, less divided and uninformed.

And when I talk about *public wisdom* I am suggesting that the public has latent wisdom that can be brought out and then spoken by its public voice—the voice of the people. I then claim that the people can and must empower their public wisdom to have real impact in the world.

I trust that by now it is clear I'm not talking about all the groups that *claim* to represent or be *the people*. I'm not talking about Tea Partiers sending a fax blast to Congress. I'm not talking about a million peace marchers in the streets protesting an impending war. I'm not talking about a Communist politburo or the U.S. Congress claiming to speak for "the people." I'm not talking about any one party, group, or institution claiming the mantle of "the people." I'm talking about an *inclusive* We the People, an *actual* We the People, a public voice arising from diverse, ordinary citizens who have bothered to really hear each other, to see each other, and then to serve their children, their communities, their country, and their world together, not only despite their differences but by using their differences creatively to speak with one inclusive and wise voice.

That public voice they create together is a voice sorely missing from today's political discourse. What we hear now is not the voice of the whole society. What we hear now is the noise of opposing voices, of partisan voices—the voices of the parts. This is all fine and good—healthy and necessary, actually—but it is *not* the voice of the people, not the inclusive voice of the whole.

Most people don't believe such an inclusive, coherent voice is possible. Some even fear it, thinking it will drown out dissent and diversity. However, those who participate in the most powerful forms of conversation— dialogue (speaking truly, and truly hearing one another), deliberation (thoroughly learning about and exploring an issue together to make a decision) and choice-creating (stepping out of roles and positions to seek together what's best for all)—know otherwise. They know that using such methods to bring forth a coherent public voice *honors and treasures diversity and dissent.* They have experienced this together. They feel its integrity in their bones. They feel its power—a power so much more powerful than any one side could ever generate separately.

15

Perhaps the main thing stopping that feeling from changing the world is that these newly realized *extraordinary citizens*—these ordinary citizens who have experienced what it is like to tap the wisdom and power of We the People through their own thoughtful conversation— don't know what to do with their newfound power and wisdom. They just know that something very different and important has happened among them.

Through this kind of process, the sleeping giant of *the people* is slowly waking up, but it doesn't quite know what to do next. In the rest of this book you will find a vision for awakening the wisdom of the people. It will invite you to consider that what's most important in democracy today is not so much mass participation by whoever shows up to voice their opinions. What's most important is engaging the *full diversity* of the population—a microcosm of We the People—with the *full diversity* of relevant information in ways that help them find *authentic common ground*. They can only do this using power-with and power-from-within. And when they do this, they create legitimate *public wisdom,* which is the foundation for a new, wiser form of democracy.

Summary

Democracy is about power.

In one sense, we already knew that. But now that sentence means much more than it ever has before. It means that democracy is about *using the right kind of power for the job,* starting with a real effort to tap into the magic and wisdom of power-with and power-from-within—including attending to the passions, interests, and needs that underlie our battles with each other. Sure, we can always fall back on the battle strategies of power-over and see who wins. But why go there first when there is so much treasure to be had by channeling our differences and common ground into a cascade of shared possibilities?

Just because our current systems of politics and governance—and economics and so many others—are designed to get us to compete doesn't mean we have to always go there. We can create new systems that help us work together more powerfully.

When I talk about coming together, even though we're all so different, I'm not talking about compromise—at least not compromise that makes us feel we've lost important things along the way. I'm talking about the shared creation of solutions and visions that the vast majority of us feel are realistic and good—even brilliant. . . .

Even wise.

CHAPTER 2

Direct Democracy, Representative Democracy, and Their Shadows

So if democracy is about power, why don't we just go for the power directly? Why not have everyone vote on everything?

As good as this sounds, it has a very dark side to it: given the systems we have, it is too easy to generate more collective stupidity and foolishness than collective intelligence and wisdom.

Think about it. There are too many issues for any given citizen to understand them all in any depth. Furthermore, nowadays every issue has so many hidden dimensions and potential side effects that our off-the-cuff opinions about them could be wildly off-base.

Many of us depend on opinion leaders, pundits, friends, or organizations that share our values to tell us what to think about the issues, to help us navigate their complexity. But almost all of them specialize in telling us only what will make us agree with them. Rare is the organization or person who fairly and knowledgeably represents the pros and cons of all sides and helps us think about the issue clearly.

If we channel all that ignorance and bias into a mass voting operation, we run the risk of generating exactly the mob rule that the Founders feared when they set up a representative democracy—that is, a republic—to keep our mass ignorance in check. The U.S. Constitution was written in a way that allowed citizens to elect leaders—mostly elite landowners—who would theoretically take the time to deliberate intelligently and figure out what should be done. And if citizens didn't like what the leaders did, they could pick someone else to replace them. They could "throw the bums out," as the saying goes.

Well, that sort of works and sort of doesn't. It turns out that many if not most of these representatives—focused as they are on getting reelected—spend more time in political gamesmanship, public relations, and fundraising (including hobnobbing with the special interests and elites who fund their election campaigns) than they do actually deliberating. And since they want to also make a good impression on the folks back home, their supposed deliberations more often than not involve what's become known as "pork"—special money or treatment for the people in their district or their supporters, even if it means undermining the common good or tacking a special amendment onto legislation about a totally different subject, just to slip it through.

As time passes, it costs more and more to get elected, and the science of political public relations more precisely targets the unconscious urges and responses of smaller and smaller "swing voter" subsets of the population. So it becomes increasingly unlikely that a politician will articulate a coherent and meaningful viewpoint that they really believe in and that actually serves the deep longings of the vast majority of their constituents. Rather, they speak in sound bites designed to trigger certain reactions in targeted voters—anger, fear, disgust—rather than promoting thoughtful opinions. And of course such reactions usually manifest as enthusiastic support for policies that favor the rich and powerful players who fund the politician's campaigns. All too often, voters end up supporting candidates and platforms that run quite counter to their own self-interest and ideals, without even realizing it.

Thus the representative democracy of our republic often generates as much "mob rule" as direct democracy does. And if simplistic forms of direct democracy were broadly instituted, the kind of degraded political public relations we see influencing voters during ballot initiatives and referendum campaigns would become the new form of co-stupidity that turns thoughtful citizens away from politics. More and more, we end up with our democracy being shaped by "the usual suspects"—the polarized partisans who show up wherever there is a chance to speak or vote—rather than by the broader wisdom that is available through the informed, collaborative engagement of the full diversity of perspectives and voices.

For those seeking a healthier, wiser democracy, the question is no longer: Which is better: direct democracy or representative democracy? The more useful questions are: What are the gifts and limitations of both direct and representative democracy? How can the gifts be strengthened and the limitations ameliorated? What is the best role they could play *together*? What else is needed that neither one of them gives us enough of?

One interesting variation on direct democracy, made possible by online electronic systems, is to allow citizens to assign someone else (a proxy) to vote for them on specific issues or under certain circumstances; they would be able withdraw their permission at any time. While open to abuse (both through hacking and by partisans collecting proxy rights like they collect petition signatures today, from people influenced by manipulative public relations campaigns), there may be secure versions that remain useful, especially locally, where answerability is tighter. But this is a footnote, for the issue of deliberation and wisdom remains.

It is clear that money and public relations have largely pushed aside real deliberation and collaboration in politics. So anything that limits the power of money and public relations in politics would help (see chapter 14). We can even get creative. Imagine, just for example, a substantial tax on campaign advertisements, which is then used to fund highly visible conversations where groups of ordinary citizens publicly interview politicians, no holds barred. Or imagine a rule whereby a legislator who was given more than a thousand dollars by an organization could not vote on any legislation concerning that organization because it would be a conflict of interest. Once we identify and prioritize the problem, there are many ways we could approach solving it.

What is the proper role of representative democracy? Let us imagine for a moment a time when our public dialogue and public choices are not being unduly manipulated by special interests. At that point it would be clearly useful to have some full-time elected officials researching, deliberating, and participating with us in making decisions on complex issues. It would be especially useful to have them bring to our attention how various issues and decisions impact each other. These important contributions could greatly enhance the people's wisdom as communities and countries wrestle with their collective affairs.

But in order to have that benefit, we need to have checks on the powerful role of representatives. We don't want our elected officials making decisions that are clearly bad for us. We don't want them ignoring us. And we don't want them neglecting or suppressing decisions that would be good for us. To prevent bad representation, it is good not only to have presidential and legislative elections (through which we can replace politicians we don't like), but also to have the more targeted instrument called *direct democracy*, in which We the People can control or bypass our representatives when we need to. But remember what I noted earlier: for direct democracy to work well, it requires that public dialogue and public choices are not unduly manipulated by special interests. This is the same requirement for representative democracy to work well.

Finally, we come to the question of what else is needed to make our democratic system work wisely enough to successfully tackle the complex problems, emerging crises, looming catastrophes, and unprecedented opportunities of our new century. My answer is *empowered public wisdom*—and you'll find out how to generate it in the rest of this book.

CHAPTER 3

Why We Need Public Wisdom

Public wisdom.

Is it asking too much to ask for wisdom—especially from the public?

No, it isn't.

Isn't wisdom a quality that we find in ancient traditions and in certain old people with much experience?

Yes, we often find wisdom in these places. But they are not the only places we find wisdom.

When I speak of public wisdom—the people's wisdom—I define *wisdom* as "the capacity to take into account what needs to be taken into account in order to produce long-term, inclusive benefits."

This is a very practical definition. When our public decisions take into account the full complexity of an issue, we can justifiably call them wise. When the public—as a whole or in the form of randomly selected "mini-publics" —engage in learning, reflecting, and talking amongst themselves in ways that consider all the factors and viewpoints related to an issue in order to make decisions that produce long-term, inclusive benefits, then we can fairly say we are generating *public wisdom.*

Today most decisions about public issues are made in ways that serve short-term and/or exclusive interests more than "the general welfare" (the U.S. Constitution's phrase for the common good). We've watched the rich getting richer with bail-outs, subsidies, low taxes, and financial deregulation. We've watched powerful teachers' unions impeding important reforms in education. We've seen lobbyists for insurance and pharmaceutical industries blocking national health care policies that the vast majority of Americans want. We've watched oil companies block climate change legislation and escape taxes and liability for oil spills. We've seen marijuana legalization blocked by corporations that run private prisons and value the "market" in nonviolent offenders. Lobbying by powerful special-interest groups seems to run the country and many states and communities. Clearly wisdom is not what we get from politics as usual.

Even when a policy is well intentioned and aimed at broad benefit, it all too often fails to take into account important factors, and those omissions then generate problematic side effects. For example, it is good to save lives by feeding the hungry and healing the sick, but we also need to keep population and consumption in check or we end up generating more hunger, disease, and environmental degradation through overpopulation. It is good to end a war, but we also need to fix some of the messes we've made in the process and to provide jobs and trauma care for returning soldiers. It is good to provide funds for rebuilding war-torn nations or aiding developing countries, but what if the money ends up in the hands of corrupt officials and sleazy businesses?

So wisdom demands both: a strong motivation to serve the general welfare over the long haul *and* a firm grounding in reality, taking account of all aspects of an issue without being blinded or biased by ideology, ignorance, laziness, or manipulation.

It would be nice if we could depend on wise philosopher kings to do all this for us. Unfortunately, such people (like all people) have a habit of being negatively affected by the attentions and privileges of power—or else dying from causes that may or may not be natural.

We've seen that the governmental structures our Founders left us—for all their brilliantly designed checks and balances—have become inadequate to restrain the abuses of power that are rampant in our current democratic constitutional republic.

We are in a time of mounting and increasingly interrelated crises—economic, political, social, and ecological. These problems will not resolve easily. The longer we go without wisely addressing them, the more complex, resistant, entangled, and dangerous they become. Their persistence and messiness have earned them the name *wicked problems* from social scientists. Many social scientists also see their development in even more dire terms: *systemic collapse.*

I join with others who see these emerging crises as signs of an impending transformation. The old systems are no longer working the ways they did. Increasingly they are creating problems and dangers rather than good lives and a better world. One way or another, something is going to shift. It is hard to imagine how that shift will be positive unless we can muster the collective wisdom to guide it in life-serving directions.

We can only do that if we make a real effort—as a society—to take into account everything that needs to be taken into account to generate long-term inclusive benefits.

We need to awaken our public wisdom. We need to engage additional sources of wisdom to enhance it. We need public power to get our public wisdom applied to public policies, programs, and budgets. And we need our public wisdom to come alive in the awareness and activities of millions of people in our communities, in our country, and in our world.

Where can we get these things?

CHAPTER 4

Public Wisdom: Its Role, Its Sources, and Its Limitations

We need public wisdom

- to advise our leaders (elected and otherwise);
- to keep officials and others in power answerable;
- to inform and advise individual citizens (especially voters);
- to awaken the public will and power of whole communities;
- to tap into and reflect on the knowledge of experts, while keeping them in their place (they need to be on tap, not on top); and, in some cases,
- to directly make some of the most important decisions our society faces.

In a democracy we, the people, are stewards of the values in our communities and country. We need to be in charge of seeing that those values govern our collective lives. But it is not always clear how those values should play out in specific circumstances, for the common good, among all our diverse neighbors. That's why we need to talk together about it. That's why we need to learn from and challenge experts and stakeholders about it. That's why we need to engage our representatives and other community and national leaders about it.

The public is where the buck stops. The public, as the collective supreme ruler of our democracy, has tremendous responsibility. The public needs to be able to find its own wisdom—*public wisdom.* This wisdom is something more than all of us individually trying to be wise, to be informed, to be good citizens. It is the wisdom that arises from our informed conversation as we—or groups of our fellow citizens who are as diverse as we are—seek shared understanding, shared solutions, and shared vision to guide the life of our shared community or society into our shared future.

If we can dependably generate real public wisdom among ourselves, there are hundreds of ways we could incorporate it into our politics, our government, and many other aspects of our community and national lives.

The Heart and Engine of Public Wisdom

At the center of our capacity to generate public wisdom are conversations among us—among *diverse* people and perspectives. All other sources of wisdom—many discussed below—are resources that can inform those conversations. But the bottom line is always us and our conversations, diverse citizens talking together productively.

We've all seen and been in conversations about public issues among diverse people and perspectives. Those conversations are usually arguments between each other, among specially selected partisans, or among whoever shows up at a meeting. Even some experts in deliberative democracy claim that deliberation among truly diverse citizens cannot be productive, based on case studies of unfacilitated or poorly facilitated citizen conversations. These are not the kinds of conversations I'm talking about here.

How conversations are set up makes all the difference in the world. This should be no surprise. Design and process are important in all sorts of situations and sectors. Different farming practices generate greater or lesser yields. Different urban arrangements make cities pleasant or alienating. Different arrangements of fuel and flame can cook your dinner or blow up a building. The same truth applies to conversations.

Diverse people talking together can result in a fistfight or a brilliant solution. To a certain extent, it depends on who the people are and how they treat each other. Given the importance of public wisdom, however, we can't afford to leave the outcomes of important public conversations to the presence or absence of maturity, civility, and enlightened wisdom in the individual participants.

This is where conversational design and facilitation come in. In Congress they have parliamentary procedure and a chairperson to keep things from going crazy. The most widely used parliamentary process in the United States, originally based on Congress's process, is *Robert's Rules of Order*. Pulled together about 140 years ago by an Army engineer, Brigadier General Henry Martyn Robert, it

31

provides a good system for maintaining order and getting productive work done in a fractious group. But it is not necessarily the best system for generating the kind of wisdom we need to address critical twenty-first-century issues.

Most of us are unfamiliar with what a wisdom-generating conversational process would look like. We're familiar with the arguments, debates, negotiations, public hearings, and lectures with question-and-answer periods that are common in public places. We're also familiar with the rambling kinds of conversation and gossip that happen across fences, over dinner tables, in bars, in online chats and blog comments, in phone calls and texting. Some of us have seen some decent deliberations using *Robert's Rules* and a few people know how to make and second a motion or an amendment, and to debate and vote according to the rules.

That's all well and good. But it's not what I'm talking about.

What Kind of Conversation Generates Public Wisdom?

Conversations that generate public wisdom offer a full spectrum of relevant perspectives that are diverse in terms of both the information made available to the participants and the views of the participants themselves—although the participants are encouraged simply to be themselves rather than represent a particular perspective or constituency. Such conversations also do the following:

- help participants discern and investigate lies and manipulation;
- ensure that every voice is really heard—and that every person *feels* well heard;
- clearly describe what the participants are being asked to do and how any results will be used;
- engage productively with differences, disturbances, and expressions of emotion;
- help participants step out of oversimplifications to creatively tackle the true complexity of real situations.

None of these things is easy to practice or provide. Our culture does not model these things for us, teach them well, or offer much support for them. But they are possible to create and facilitate, even with people who have little natural capacity to provide them for themselves. There are dozens of ways to do each and every one of them. While specific methods may be better or worse for particular purposes in particular situations, the factors in the above list are among the most vital determinants of how much public wisdom we can produce.

Notice that all of them have to do with helping the whole group work together to take into account everything that needs to be taken into account in order to serve the long-term well-being of their whole community, society, and world.

The Inside Secret

Part of what makes these conversations capable of generating wisdom is that deep inside every person is a realm of genetic, physiological, emotional, mental, social, and often spiritual common ground that they share with every other human being.

In other words, because we are all human beings—and despite all our differences—we have a tremendous amount in common. Virtually all of us have experienced pleasure and pain, joy and anger, birth and death, loving and hating, hunger and satisfaction, beauty and ugliness, and freedom and oppression. Most of us feel more at home and at peace in situations where we are appreciated for who we really are, where we can contribute in real ways, where we feel safe and respected, and where our needs are understood and met. Yes, we have different cultures, classes, genders, political opinions, abilities, races, and experiences. But somewhere deep inside, we know what it feels like to be a human being in this world. And we can reconnect to that knowledge in quality conversation with others.

Much of this commonality of experience is limited to our common humanness. But other aspects arise from our relationship to other forms of life, especially our expressive hairy cousins, the other mammals: the cats, dogs, chimpanzees, horses, polar bears, and all the rest. Because of this we can experience a certain empathy and resonance with animals and plants—some of us more than others, but all of us to some degree. We know what it feels like to be tortured or pleasured, even to an animal. Research recently disclosed the existence of "mirror neurons": because most of us have these in our brains, when we see a person or animal being hurt, part of us feels the same pain they are feeling. This is natural compassion.

To some degree this felt and factual commonality connects us to all other forms of life, for we are living beings. We share the earth as our living space: the sky above, the ground below, the rhythms of seasons and biological functions, the flowing of water and air (including the vital cycles of oxygen and carbon dioxide), and the forests, caves, and structures that are homes to living beings of all kinds. All these things we share with all life. Even in our manufactured worlds of concrete, glass, metal, plastic, abstractions, and special effects, these natural realities call to us and can move us in deep ways. We can even imagine—however inexactly—what life might be like for an ant or a crow.

Some even say we share a common mind; a collective consciousness; a shared spirit, soul, or "ground of being." Regardless of how any of these may or may not be true, we needn't go any further than our physical, biological, and social creatureliness to realize our kinship and commonality. This realization can be a profound source of wisdom because it emerges from the truth of our fellowship with each other and all life, which, when we take it seriously, guides us to seek long-term benefits for all. It can call us back to these realities when we get lost in artificial divisions and disconnections.

When we are grounded in this deep-shared experience more than in our different ideologies, cultures, and political positions, we rediscover our common humanity and aliveness. That prepares us to identify and articulate the common good, to believe that it matters and is possible, and to feel inspired to bring it about in the real world.

By giving us the challenge to pursue the common good in the face of all our differences, and then helping us to really hear each other, powerful conversational approaches lead us progressively into what I call the *core commons* of our life. Going there stimulates a shift in us, a shift that is essential to our individual and collective discovery of our wisdom and power as We the People. We realize that so much more and better is possible than ever before.

Some people encourage me to talk more about the spiritual dimensions of high-quality conversational approaches. For me, though, there isn't much to say beyond what I've said here. Whatever connects us to our core commons—the heart and soul of our connection to each other and the world—is spiritual to me. And high-quality conversation draws us into that connection in a very clean and simple way, with no need for any spiritual language or sectarian or esoteric beliefs or practices.

So this is the fundamental tool: diverse people interacting in conversations that help them ground in their natural common humanity and life. When we are successful at that, we are well on the road to group wisdom.

But there's more.

Seeking Greater Wisdom

As we pursue public wisdom we should always ask: what else can we do to make these conversations more wise? In particular: how can we reach beyond our limited ways of thinking? Our society works very hard to put us in boxes and frames and then to convince us that they are real and complete, that we should stay in them and never think of stepping outside. But we *must* leave them if we wish to see the bigger pictures that will give us wisdom. Here are some ways to do that:

Creatively engage diverse forms of intelligence. Help people use their full human capacities—including reason, emotion, intuition, humor, and movement, as well as aesthetic and spiritual sensibilities, capacities, and activities. Different people have different ways of learning, engaging, and expressing themselves, and these differences are among the most valuable to respect and use creatively.

Consult global wisdom traditions and broadly shared ethics. Ethical principles common to most major religions and philosophies provide time-tested wisdom. We can augment these with what humanity has learned more recently through science and global dialogue about what serves human needs and happiness. Two good resources for this are the Council for a Parliament of the World Religions and the Universal Declaration of Human Rights. Nonviolent Communication and Chilean economist Manfred Max-Neef provide deep insight into universal human needs. (Note: It is fine for conversational participants to be individually informed and guided by their own faith traditions and practices. It is also often useful for spiritual or religious groups to bring prayer, meditation, or other sacred practices into their dialogues and deliberations. But there is good reason for the separation of church and state. So in inclusive democratic conversations pursuing the common good, we need to stick to broadly held ethical principles, like the Golden Rule, which shows up in virtually every major religious tradition. If a spiritually deepening practice is desired in the course of a public conversation among diverse citizens, simple silence for a few minutes can serve well, across virtually all traditions.)

Seek guidance from natural patterns. Wisdom is embedded in nature, in organisms, in natural forms and processes, and in the dynamics of evolution, providing a vast reservoir of insight and know-how tapped by today's scientists and engineers, often standing on the shoulders of ancient tribal and agricultural cultures. Among the good resources on this are biomimicry, the study of how nature solves engineering problems, and permaculture, the study of how to design fruitful natural systems from scratch. Both sciences offer many insights into how we can enhance community and societal health.

Apply systems thinking. Systems thinking can help people understand underlying causes and take into account how things are interrelated, how wholes and parts influence each other through power relations, resonance, feedback dynamics, flows, motivating purposes, and life-shaping narratives, habits, and structures. A good resource on this is the work of Donella Meadows. Her many articles and her book *Thinking in Systems* are compelling and easy to understand.

Think about the big picture and the long term. Wisdom grows as we step out of limiting perspectives to understand (and creatively use) histories and energies from the past, current contexts and trends, future ramifications and needs, larger and smaller scales, and other mind-expanding perspectives. Briefing materials, metaphors, stories, and visual presentations can introduce participants to such larger contexts. Exercises can invite participants to step into expanded views—using role-playing, for example, to step into others' shoes, or visioning to step into the future, or brainstorming to step into wildly creative perspectives and possibilities.

Seek agreements that are truly inclusive. To the extent lots of people contribute to, engage with, and believe in an agreement, that agreement will wisely address what needs to be addressed and will get implemented well. At the very least, don't be satisfied with mere majority voting, which depends on majority domination and leaves a significant minority dissatisfied. Dig deeper into shared values and needs. Every step of the way, seek out people's concerns and take them seriously to see if they can be satisfied in ways that move group support closer to a supermajority (67 percent or more) or a consensus or breakthrough that all participants are pleased with. Note that shallow, reluctant agreements and compromises—as well as agreements based on deals irrelevant to the issue being discussed—may get results, but those results won't be wise.

Compromises and similar strategies arise from the group's inability to actually address what needs to be addressed to produce a truly inclusive resolution of the issue—namely, their differences and the important realities hidden within those differences.

Release the potential of hidden assets and positive possibilities. In addressing a situation, we cover more ground and inspire more support and participation if we notice and creatively engage energies and resources that already exist in the situation and tap the power of people's aspirations, which often show up at the rough edges, on the margins. Among the good resources for this are Appreciative Inquiry, Positive Deviance, Asset-Based Community Development, and Dynamic Facilitation, each of which has its own powerful approach for evoking positive possibilities from problems and conflicts. (See appendix 1 for more information on these and other processes mentioned in this book.)

Encourage healthy self-organization and learning. Any situation or system contains people, experience, ideas, and capacities that can help those involved solve problems and self-organize in healthy ways—if they are invited and supported in doing so. Here are some ways to do this: Create an atmosphere of participation and collaboration. Ask powerful questions. Elicit crowdsourced ideas and resources. Offer incentives. Play games designed to bring out and explore the dynamics of the situation. Bring vibrant, empowered democracy into it. Convene World Café conversations (see page 112) and Open Space conferences (see page 114) to provide juicy approaches to help a group or community explore and solve its own problems and pursue what the people involved really want to do together. (These two powerful methods are particularly easy to convene and facilitate.)

Make information more accessible and meaningful as knowledge. As noted earlier, information presented to citizen deliberators should be diverse and true. In addition, both the information and its significance should be readily understandable. Simple language, narrative forms, and meaningful visual and audiovisual presentations can help tremendously. The work of Edward Tufte explores how to present data in meaningful visual ways, and argument mapping and framing for deliberation cover the presentation of diverse perspectives in ways that make them easy to understand and compare. Journalists can also help clarify the larger stories that make useful meaning out of isolated pieces of data.

Do it again. Redundancy and iteration are powerful patterns in nature. *Redundancy* means having more than enough of something. Having an extra hand, arm, foot, eye, lung, and ear not only means that they can work together but that if we lose one, we still have the other. Asking three friends about a car repair shop tends to produce more useful information than asking only one friend. Doing three comparable public deliberations and comparing the results is more likely to produce wisdom than doing only one. *Iteration* means doing things again, informed by feedback from earlier attempts. Wise people notice the results of their actions and act accordingly, correcting their errors. Likewise, a one-time public process can generate a certain amount of public wisdom, but doing a similar activity every three months or every year increases the chance that each new iteration will learn from the previous ones and from the real-world effects of their earlier recommendations.

No Guarantees, but Good Chances . . .

Our definition of public wisdom is based on the obvious and painful fact that when we fail to take something important into account, it comes back to bite us—perhaps not immediately, but sooner or later, in one way or another. Foolish, ill-considered decisions tend to leave us with worse problems than we had before. Wiser decisions tend to create fewer bad outcomes because they take into account more of what—and who—is most relevant and important.

In practice, though, we don't really know how wise a decision is until long after it is implemented. After all, it is the long-term results that make it wise, by definition. The more "wicked" the problem, the more we get to face this sobering reality; the problem's complexity makes it that much harder to predict what will happen. To really know whether a decision is wise, we have to wait and see.

However, just because we can't be *certain* a decision is wise at the time it is made, doesn't mean we're helpless. There is much we can do before, during, and after we make a decision to make it more likely that it will be wise. Our definition of public wisdom—considering together what actually needs to be taken into account to produce long-term broad benefits—implies guidelines and approaches like those described in this chapter. These practices lead us to consider "more of the whole." So the more of them we incorporate into our citizen engagement, politics, and governance—and the more effectively we do each one—the more likely it will be that we will generate public wisdom.

CHAPTER 5

Citizenship and the Random Selection of Ad Hoc Mini-Publics

Two of the main obstacles to the effectiveness and wisdom of our democracy are (a) the time demands of responsible citizenship and (b) the side effects of power, especially corruption. These factors block our capacity to address our public issues well, and they frustrate efforts to elect better lawmakers and to get more people involved in public affairs. This is obviously a dangerous combination.

Ordinary people simply don't have time to get informed on all the issues. So they delegate their decision-making power to politicians. Most politicians, by the nature of their jobs, tend to have big egos, big ambitions, and big bank accounts (or at least the ability to please rich and powerful supporters). These qualities lend themselves to conflicts of interest and corruption as our politician travels his or her path to power, and especially when he or she has finally achieved that power and wants to use it and hold on to it. Rare is the politician who doesn't want to be reelected—and reelection usually requires a significant amount of money and some compromise of integrity. From early on, politicians are surrounded by powerful special interests that gravitate to centers of concentrated power, bringing a lot of money, persuasion, and demands with them. It is hard to ignore them when your political career is at stake.

Even when a politician's integrity remains mostly intact, he or she may soon become habituated to the privileges, obeisance, assumptions, and fellowship that go along with power and the elite culture in which he or she has become embedded. Furthermore, the intensely competitive atmosphere of business-as-usual politics—with its ongoing strategic pressures and often ruthless attacks by opponents, the press, and adversarial interests—cannot help but have an impact.

All this does not add up to an environment that supports integrity, authenticity, openness, and—unfortunately—wisdom. Also unfortunately, these phenomena get more intense the higher one goes in the political system, as social power becomes more concentrated and the stakes get higher.

Two strategies can help disrupt these dynamics: random selection and limited time in office. If decision-makers are randomly selected and therefore unpredictable, neither they nor special interests can prepare to manipulate their power for personal or partisan gain. The lobbyists don't know ahead of time whom to lobby. And then, when decision-makers are in power, their brevity in office (which is sometimes institutionalized as "term limits" or enforced by a "recall" process) gives less time for them to be lobbied and for the competitive pressures of politics and the dynamics of elite culture to erode their personalities and principles.

Putting these two strategies together creates a new possibility for all citizens in a democracy. They can delegate some their decision-making power to temporary panels of randomly selected ordinary citizens. As noted earlier, such ad hoc panels are not imaginary; they have been convened and tested many times. They are like trial juries, but they deal with public issues and policies instead of crimes and personal injuries. They can be plugged into the existing political system in various ways (which are covered in the next chapter), or they can—and nowadays usually do— operate outside of that system.

In addition to being more resistant to corruption, such panels constitute microcosms of the citizenry—what pollsters call mini-publics. Individually, panel members are more like their fellow citizens than politicians are. In fact, they *are* ordinary citizens. And together—because of the way they are chosen—they embody the diversity, values, and life experience of the whole community from which they were selected. Note how different this is both from elected politicians and from participatory approaches that are based on whoever shows up.

Used in this way—to create a microcosm of a community—random selection helps keep democratic processes fair and vibrant. Every citizen has an equal chance of being selected, and being selected is a great honor and responsibility shared by all.

Random selection is not a wild new idea. It has a long and interesting history. Roughly 2,500 years ago, Athens's democracy was run with a mix of direct democracy (all the citizens voting on everything in a big assembly) and random selection (they drew lots to fill 90 percent of the official positions in government). They used elections only to choose their top generals and to fill Athens's top financial positions. They considered random selection fundamental to democracy—a sacred embodiment of fairness and citizen responsibility for the welfare of the whole community.

Most significant for our purposes here, Athens innovated a form of randomly selected mini-public responsible for recommending public policy. Their *boule* contained five hundred members chosen by lot from the whole body of citizens over thirty years of age. These members served one-year terms. Among other important duties—including qualifying and reviewing officeholders—they reviewed and prepared measures for the vote of the citizenry in the assembly.

In the past forty years people around the world have been experimenting with new forms of mini-publics containing from only twelve up to two hundred randomly selected citizens for facilitated deliberations lasting from several days to several weeks spread over several months. Hundreds of these kinds of ad hoc mini-publics have been convened, but few have been set up to have an institutionalized impact on policy. Yet their very existence creates a new, deeper form of citizenship than we're used to, and a new, more inclusive public voice in the political discourse.

With time and support, the ordinary folks chosen for mini-publics perform a near-ideal act of citizenship: They learn about an issue in depth from all sides. They discuss it with folks who think differently than they do. And in those conversations with their fellow citizens and with experts and stakeholders, they come to informed, thoughtful conclusions about what should be done about the issue. They become not only lay experts on the issue but an informed, deliberative microcosm of the whole public. They speak with a certain legitimate authority about what the citizenry would want if everyone could and would engage in a comparably sophisticated act of collective citizenship. As with trial juries, they speak with the voice of the whole—both symbolically and, if they are convened properly, actually.

Speaking personally, I am one of the millions of citizens who just can't keep track of the hundreds of issues and proposals. I am tired of the political spin and partisan battles that confuse me about what's really going on and what's really at stake. I often yearn for groups like these citizen mini-publics to advise me on *all* the issues I read about and vote on. I long for them to have a powerful role in our society's official decision making. I imagine what it would be like to have this informed, thoughtful voice of the people present in *all* our public discourse, speaking not just to citizens like me but powerfully to politicians, pundits, corporations, and public officials.

How different it would be to have members of such a panel, when they have completed their work, appear on talk shows to discuss what they came up with and what it was like to learn about the issue, talk with each other, and *act!* How risky it would be for a talk show host to be a jerk with them. They wouldn't be like other guests. The talk show host would be in conversation with We the People—and in a democracy, you don't mess with an authentic, powerful We the People!

Of course, such an implicitly powerful institution, even if randomly selected and temporary, requires thoughtful design and procedure to help it be wise and sustainable. It shouldn't be too large or too small—or deliberate for too long or too short a time. Like a trial jury, it needs legal and procedural safeguards to protect it from manipulation. It needs dependable information—and help understanding that information. It needs good facilitation, and we need to ensure that the facilitation can't be abused. (Juries handle the issue of abuse by having no trained facilitators at all. While this reduces the chance of external abuse and manipulation through the facilitator's power, it also increases the likelihood of internal abuse, manipulation, and polarization among the participants themselves and reduces the chance that real wisdom will emerge. Think about the bullet points in the previous chapter on generating wisdom and imagine how little of that would happen in most groups of ordinary people talking together without guidance. It seems to me that we need to use expert facilitation.) In addition to those challenges, most existing forms of citizen deliberative councils are expensive—at least for grassroots community groups and cash-strapped local governments—ranging from tens to hundreds of thousands of dollars. So we need to develop less expensive versions that can still generate legitimate public wisdom.

These limitations, cautions, and challenges are no reason to not promote public wisdom processes with all the energy we've got. They are design issues. We need to design these councils well in the first place. Then, as they are institutionalized and become more powerful, they join the list of democratic institutions—like elections and freedoms—that we need to protect. Public wisdom, like liberty, requires both good systemic design and constant vigilance.

This is probably a good point to highlight what a different vision of democracy this is. To most people democracy involves thousands or millions of citizens discussing, advocating, and voting on public issues. Nowadays when these citizens act together, they almost always act in partisan associations—political parties, advocacy groups, and so on—to elect candidates or push for public policies they favor. The latest trends in revitalizing democracy focus on mass participation—getting as many people as possible to do these things—to talk, to vote, to volunteer, to protest—the more the merrier. Mass public conversations, voter registration drives, online citizen input websites, voter information websites, and other approaches seek to involve more and more individual citizens in informed civic activity.

This is all very important work. But notice how different it is from a focus on (a) public wisdom and (b) generating and empowering a legitimate, inclusive, informed, and coherent voice of *the whole people* that can articulate that wisdom and push it into public policy. As odd as it may seem, public wisdom doesn't depend on mass public participation. It depends on engaging just enough people to adequately embody the diversity of the population, and then giving them support to generate wise understandings and recommendations about what the rest of us and our representatives should do about the issues we face.

In a sense, such mini-public deliberations are a scaling up of a practice even older than the Athenian *boule*—the ancient tribal practice of sitting around a "council fire" considering issues of consequence facing the tribe. As my colleague Rosa Zubizaretta has said, "Our indigenous ancestors knew that to meet in a circle is sacred, whether we are doing so to communicate with other dimensions of time, space, and being, or whether we are doing so for the equally numinous purpose of communicating with one another, talking and listening, witnessing and presencing, until there is 'nothing left but the obvious truth.'" Sitting in council is a deep-rooted part of our social DNA. But how do we do this sacred duty with millions of people— millions of diverse people with different beliefs, cultures, and interests?

Unfortunately, involving millions of people in any particular deliberative activity reduces the likelihood that a wise, inclusive, coherent, and legitimate voice of the people will emerge from it—unless the activity includes citizen deliberative councils. Ideally, the wisdom generated by such well-supported mini-publics would inform the citizenship, conversations, and activism of the rest of us, thereby helping us to be collectively wise in the directions we take our society and world.

Creating the capacity for public wisdom in twenty-first-century America is no greater a challenge than that faced by our country's original Founders. But this is *our* task, *our* calling. *We* are the revolutionary founders of this new democracy—a democracy that will have an impact at least as great, and probably greater, than the impact their revolution had on the world almost 250 years ago.

PART TWO

Making It Happen—
Some Pieces of the Puzzle

CHAPTER 6

Citizen Deliberative Councils:
Their Character, Variety, and History

Without deliberation we don't get public wisdom. Even in an individual, wisdom does not come from experience or teachings alone. Individuals must reflect on their experiences and what others have told them; notice connections, consequences, and contradictions; and must test what they believe against challenges in their minds, in conversations, and, above all, in life in order to derive sound, beneficial knowledge over time.

In a citizen deliberative council the experience being considered is the diverse experience of its members, and the teachings are the diverse facts and lessons provided by various experts. It is precisely the diversity of these things that enables them to support the emergence of wisdom. Instead of wisdom deriving from making sense of varied moments over time in one person's life, it derives from making sense of the diversity of life experiences and lessons in a mixed group and the diversity of information and perspectives gleaned from fair full-spectrum briefings and diverse expert witnesses. Instead of this being mulled over in the lone mind of an individual, it is mulled over in the minds of a dozen or a hundred people in respectful, creative conversation. Whatever coherent understanding emerges from that process has broader applicability and benefit because of the diversity of knowledge and experience from which it was drawn, and the fact that that diversity was not suppressed but instead honored and used creatively.

The popular "wisdom of crowds" idea—that the aggregated responses of many independent people generates better answers than any one of them would, or even than experts would—is sometimes useful for crowdsourced estimates and predictions. But it does not generate true wisdom as described in this book. That requires high-quality deliberative conversation among diverse people.

My definition of *deliberation* in this work is "thorough, thoughtful consideration of how to best address an issue or situation, covering a wide range of information, perspectives, and potential consequences of diverse approaches."

Deliberation can be done in any number of ways, from extensive rigorous reflection to dynamic, creative interaction. The key feature in relation to *public wisdom* is the thoroughness of the process: does it help participants take into account what needs to be considered for long-term success and broad benefit? Full information, critical thinking, reflection, creativity, emotion, vision, stories, and dynamic interaction all play important roles in this.

How do we generate public wisdom with, by, and for a whole population?

Citizen deliberative councils have a unique and pivotal role to play in bringing public wisdom into the formal functioning of politics and governance. As noted in the previous chapter, these temporary councils of citizens are designed to reflect the diversity of the population, so when they are convened to deliberate on public concerns and provide guidance for officials and the public, they have a special legitimacy—the legitimacy of We the People, the rightful source of guidance and power in a democracy.

The primary quality that makes them different from other democratic forms that claim to represent We the People—that is, elected representatives, populist partisan groups, public forums open to whoever shows up, and public opinion polls—is the fact that citizen deliberative councils are a true microcosm of the whole society, and they are undertaking a near-ideal act of interactive citizenship on behalf of that society. They call forth, embody, and ultimately promote the latent public wisdom of the whole population.

There are many varieties of citizen deliberative council—which will be described later in this chapter—but they all share one purpose and eight characteristics. The purpose of a citizen deliberative council is to inform officials and the public of what the people as a whole would really want if they were to thoroughly learn about a public concern or issue, carefully think about it, and productively talk it over with each other.

The eight characteristics shared by every current form of citizen deliberative council are as follows:

■ It is an organized face-to-face assembly.
■ It is made up of twelve to two hundred citizens selected

59

randomly (and usually demographically) so that their collective diversity fairly reflects the profile of the larger community from which they were drawn. (In this context, "community" means any coherent civic population, whether a block, a citizens' organization, a city, a province, a country, or any other such public grouping. And I use the word "citizen" here to mean simply an inhabitant of a community, although others may legitimately use it to mean "an officially recognized member of a country" or "a politically involved member of a community" such as a registered voter.)

- It is convened temporarily, for a specified time, usually a few days or weeks of actual meetings, sometimes distributed over several weeks or months.

- Its members deliberate as peers, setting aside any other roles or statuses they may have for the brief duration of their deliberations, after which they return to their previous lives in their community.

- It has an explicit mandate to address a specific public situation, issue, concern, budget, group of proposals or candidates, or other public matter, including the general state and aspirations of the community.

- It uses forms of dialogue and deliberation, usually facilitated, that enable its diverse members to really hear each other, to expand and deepen their understanding of the issues involved, and to engage together to identify the best ways their community might address them.

- Its deliberations are informed by inclusive, balanced briefing materials and, usually, interviews with, testimony from, and/or conversations with diverse experts, advocates, and other stakeholders involved with the matter under consideration.

▪ At its conclusion, it releases its findings and recommendations to its convening authority, concerned officials, the media, the electorate, and/or the larger community from which its members came—and then it disbands.

Ideally, the report stimulates further community dialogue, some of which may be purposefully convened and/or reported on as part of the overall process.

Citizen deliberative councils in most current forms have no permanent or official power except the power of legitimacy and (hopefully) widely publicized common-sense solutions to compelling public problems. This book considers ways to expand their influence.

Although few people realize it, hundreds of these groups of ordinary citizens have been formally convened all over the world during the last forty years. All together they have involved tens of thousands of people in both developed and developing nations. They are happening in many places right now. Here are four examples covered in my book *The Tao of Democracy*, just to give you a taste:

▪ In India, poor farmers held a deliberative council investigating approaches to economic development. They decided they wanted to continue and improve their self-reliant food and farming and to control their communities' resources.

▪ In Great Britain, sixteen randomly selected citizens

who were convened to deliberate about plant biotechnology studied the issue and cross-examined opposing experts in a public forum. They came to consensus about the benefits, risks, harmful marketing practices, and need for regulation of biotech companies and biotech development.

- In Australia, suburbanites deliberated on what to do about pollution and erosion associated with rainwater that was wrecking their beaches. They created a program of low-cost, low-tech, readily doable all-sector interventions addressing the problem at its many local sources with participatory local action.

- In America, eighteen ordinary citizens became expert enough in a few days to tell Twin Cities municipal authorities how to deal with the area's solid waste disposal. They wanted more sustainable practices.

In every case, ordinary people reviewed the facts and came up with common-sense solutions. The idea that we could empower such groups to have a positive impact on our major public problems and crises offers possibilities for a positive future to replace the dire prospects and heartbreaking visions currently rampant in our struggling society.

Citizen Deliberative Councils Contrasted with Two Similar Approaches

Deliberative Polling® and 21st Century Town Meetings® are two fashionable deliberative processes that bear some resemblance to citizen deliberative councils and have their own place in efforts to build empowered public wisdom. A brief comparison provides useful insight about them and where they fit.

A Deliberative Poll convenes two hundred to six hundred randomly selected people who have been surveyed about a public issue and then further informed on the issue through balanced briefing materials. They gather for a weekend in which they question competing experts about the issue. They are then resurveyed and the results are compared. The results often show significant shifts in individual views. Since a primary purpose of the exercise is public education, the briefing materials are publicly available and their deliberations often receive television coverage. A primary difference between Deliberative Polls and citizen deliberative councils is that the former does not seek to create a coherent public policy recommendation, but rather to inform and demonstrate shifts in public opinion. Although its large size, brief meeting time, highly choreographed process, and lack of mandate for a coherent outcome reduce its ability to generate public wisdom, it is often a great introduction to deliberation. Participants tend to leave the event excited about what transpired, public officials are often impressed, and the viewing public finds the process fascinating and informative.

While 21st Century Town Meetings are open to anyone, they are organized with demographically targeted recruitment. They convene five hundred to five thousand people for one to two days of public deliberation at facilitated tables of ten to twelve participants who earlier received briefing materials. Each table has a "scribe" with a computer through which the table wirelessly reports its collective responses to preset questions at scheduled intervals. A "theme team" condenses the responses into summary statements, which are then projected on giant screens viewable by all participants, who vote on them through wireless keypads (which are also used for demographic and other straw polls during the event). These huge public events tend to attract considerable media coverage as well as attention from officials, who, along with the participants, receive a printed report at the event's conclusion. Similarly to the Deliberative Poll, the immense size of 21st Century Town Meetings, the usually preestablished choices they offer, the choreographed scheduling of deliberative activity (necessary to keep all the tables on the same page), the boxing of participant ideas into votable bullet points, and the often rushed process (with twenty to thirty minutes for ten people to have an equal say on a complex aspect of the issue and report the results) reduce its ability to generate true public wisdom. But these events, too, often evoke widespread excitement by most participants and viewers.

The smaller size and usually longer duration of citizen deliberative councils provide an opportunity to delve into issues in greater depth with outside experts and stakeholders as well as with each other. This deeper deliberation supports their mission of producing well-considered, coherent recommendations that contain a significant measure of public wisdom. However, they usually lack the media visibility and broad impact of Deliberative Polls and 21st Century Town Meetings.

I see Deliberative Polls and 21st Century Town Meetings as valuable resources (a) to introduce many citizens and public officials to the value and vitality of citizen deliberation; (b) to show citizens that their voices can be heard and matter; and (c) ultimately to help large numbers of people engage with a public issue, both before a citizen deliberative council is held and/or after it, reviewing its conclusions.

The History and Variety of Citizen Deliberative Councils

Citizen deliberative councils were first pioneered by the late German innovator Peter Dienel, who created *Planning Cells,* or *Planungszellen,* in January 1971. Planning Cells involve several separate twenty-five-member, jury-like "cells" all simultaneously considering the same issue in different geographic regions. The conclusions of the diverse cells are collected, compared, and then compiled into one "citizen report" by the organizers. Once the participants approve the report, it is presented to the sponsor, the media, and other interested parties. The first Planning Cells were held in 1971 in Germany and a few dozen more have been held since.

In April 1971 the most widely used form of citizen deliberative council, the *Citizens Jury,* was created. Citizens Juries involve twelve to twenty-four citizens, chosen by random stratified sampling (which involves demographic selection from a large random pool of citizens), interviewing experts and deliberating for three to five days. The form was conceived by American political scientist Ned Crosby as part of an academic inquiry about how a community might determine its most ethical solutions to moral dilemmas. (Crosby and Dienel were unaware of each other's work until 1985, when they met and soon discovered that they both spoke German and English and both had mothers and daughters named Elisabeth, the latter born a week apart in 1963!)

In 1974 Crosby and several civic leaders founded the Jefferson Center in Minneapolis, Minnesota, to research and develop the Citizens Jury process (along with another process called "Extended Policy Discussion," which was designed to clarify disagreements between experts on public policy matters in a way that would be useful for legislators). The first Citizens Jury on an issue was in 1974 and the first to examine candidates for office was in 1976. In 1984 a Citizens Jury was conducted for the first time with government sponsorship. As of this writing, the Jefferson Center has organized thirty-two Citizens Juries. The integrity of the Citizens Jury process is integral to its design, including transparency, on-going evaluations, and final reports written by the participants. Reports on all Jefferson Center Citizens Juries and a complete manual on conducting this form of citizen deliberation are available free on the Jefferson Center website, www.jeffersoncenter.org.

The Citizens Jury model was picked up by the British

think tank, Institute for Public Policy Research, leading to its widespread use in Britain. The British, German, and American efforts subsequently spread around the world. Many other people have since used this method. In its many variations, the Citizens Jury is the most widely used and thoroughly tested and reviewed model of citizen deliberative council in the world, and it has inspired many creative applications and versions.

More than a decade after Crosby and Dienel's innovations, another form of citizen deliberative council was instituted in Denmark. This model, called *Consensus Conferences,* consists of about eighteen randomly selected citizens who study an assigned issue and then take testimony from experts in an open public hearing. The group, with the help of a facilitator, then comes to a consensus and releases its report at a press conference. Since the mid-1980s, occasional Consensus Conferences have been convened by an office of the Danish parliament to review controversial technological issues being considered for legislation. In addition to the Danes' official Consensus Conferences, a couple dozen have been held unofficially elsewhere in the world.

The next major development came from a surprising source. One weekend in June 1991, *Maclean's* magazine— Canada's glossy newsweekly—convened a dozen Canadians in a resort north of Toronto. These folks had been scientifically chosen so that together they represented all the major sectors of public opinion and demographics in their deeply divided country. Despite their firmly held and often opposing beliefs, each of these people was interested in dialogue with people whose views differed from theirs. That dialogue was facilitated by "the guru of conflict resolution," Harvard University law professor Roger Fisher, coauthor of the classic *Getting to Yes,* and two colleagues.

Despite the fact that they'd never really listened to the viewpoints and experiences of others so unlike themselves, despite the tremendous time pressure (they had three days to develop a consensus vision for Canada), and despite being continuously watched by a camera crew from Canadian television (who recorded the event for a special hour-long public affairs program), these ordinary citizens succeeded in their mission. Their effort was extensively covered by *Maclean's* in their special "People's Verdict" issue—a fact so significant that it will be discussed in more detail in the next chapter. Unfortunately, *Maclean's* never repeated this pioneering exercise in citizen engagement.

In the early 1980s, consultant Jim Rough developed a powerfully creative form of problem solving and conflict resolution he called *Dynamic Facilitation.* At the beginning of the process, participants address their thoughts and feelings to the facilitator, who "reflects" them back in ways that ensure each speaker feels fully heard, including recording their contributions on chart pads labeled "problem statements," "possible solutions," "concerns," and "data." When anyone complains about something, the facilitator asks (after reflecting the complaint), "What do you think should be done about that?" or "If you were in charge, what would you do about it?"—channeling participants' thinking toward solving the problem without privileging any particular solution, just recording them all on the "possible solutions" chart pad. If someone starts to argue with or invalidate what another participant has said, the facilitator asks, with real curiosity, "What's your concern?"—and, after reflecting and recording his or her concern, asks what the conflicted person would do about it. This aspect of Dynamic Facilitation—translating conflict into concerns—composts antagonism into creativity.

As all the ideas and emotions participants brought with them into the session are well heard and recorded, the group becomes increasingly aware of the full complexity their diverse views add up to. At the same time— since they feel heard and have witnessed others being well heard—they are more open than when they walked in. Increasingly the group's attention moves from arguing and asserting to thinking cocreatively about the "mess"— the full complexity of the situation—they have generated together. They're thinking, "Oh my, how are *we* going to solve this?" and they start to generate new possible solutions and new angles on the problem. As this spirit comes to dominate the discussion, the group begins to make breakthroughs until a big collective *ah-ha!* comes— usually around something no one of them had thought before they came in the room. There is no "decision," as such, but more of a shared perception of what's needed, a "co-sensing."

This approach—which has mainly been used in corporations, nonprofits, and public institutions—engenders a quality of conversation Rough calls *choice-creating*. Although Rough doesn't consider choice-creating to be deliberation, I believe it fits the definition at the beginning of this chapter—albeit in a far more dynamic way than other forms of deliberation. As you may gather from the description above, his process is deeply creative and nonlinear, following the group's energy rather than any predetermined course or agenda—and it is extremely powerful.

The choice-creating conversations about public issues that Rough witnessed in his Dynamic Facilitation trainings inspired his 1993 innovation of the *Wisdom Council process*. In a Wisdom Council, one or two dozen citizens chosen through pure random selection come together for a few days with no agenda. Their job is to reflect on how their community is doing, including its needs and dreams. They may identify issues, solutions, questions, new directions, or anything else. They come up with a consensus statement—a sort of citizens' "state of the union" address—which they deliver to the community in a public meeting. (Note that the political logic of the Wisdom Council, if not the exact process, is remarkably similar to the *Maclean's* "People's Verdict" effort, about which Rough was unaware.) In a Wisdom Council *process* a new Wisdom Council is convened every three to twelve months. Given their simplicity and their ability to catalyze a spirit of We the People, Wisdom Councils will be given special strategic attention in chapter 10.

Since Wisdom Councils are not designed to deal with

an assigned issue, some dynamic facilitators wondered if Dynamic Facilitation could be used in an issue-oriented process like a Citizens Jury. At first Rough balked, because, in his view, the randomly selected members of a Wisdom Council were essentially We the People, and you don't tell We the People what to talk about; they decide for themselves.

Over the years, however, he and leading colleagues, notably Rosa Zubizarreta (who collaborated with me on *The Tao of Democracy*), began developing a powerful form of citizen deliberative council they called a Creative Insight Council (CIC). In this, one or two dozen randomly selected citizens are convened to explore a situation or proposal in a dynamically facilitated choice-creating conversation. Experts, stakeholders, and partisans on the issue are also included at the beginning, usually as witnesses or resource people (as in a Citizens Jury), and at the end they receive and comment on the CIC's results. The process is designed to generate new and potentially better ways to address the situation, not necessarily to work out detailed proposals. While still under development and tried only a few times, CICs are one of the most promising innovations in the field. I think they would be especially valuable if the CIC's initial findings, instead of being the end of the process, went to to the experts and officials to craft a new proposal, which would then be returned to the reconvened CIC for consideration in a choice-creating conversation—back and forth in an iterative manner until something solid evolved that really worked well for all concerned. One other possible variation that might be quite productive—if the experts and partisans were willing to stick it out and the facilitation were strong—would be to have them fully included in the entire choice-creating conversation.

Another new form of citizen deliberative council is the *Citizens' Assembly*. Perhaps the largest and most empowered CDC so far was the Citizens' Assembly on Electoral Reform held in British Columbia, Canada, in 2004. This panel of 160 citizens (one man and one woman randomly selected from each legislative district, plus two First Nations members) was convened to study and make recommendations on electoral reform. They met every other weekend for ten months—hearing expert testimony, holding fifty public forums, examining 1,603 written submissions from the public, and deliberating—generating creative recommendations which were then submitted to British Columbia's voters as a referendum.

The legislation that established this British Columbian Citizens' Assembly specified that if their recommendations were approved by 60% of the voters, they would become law. Since the 2005 vote in favor was only 57.7%—albeit with majorities in 77 of the 79 districts—the measure failed. A second referendum in 2009 also failed to pass. But the Citizens' Assembly process has generated much interest worldwide and been replicated in several other locations. It has also helped highlight another key aspect of citizen deliberative councils: engaging the public at large with the process and its results.

Discrepancies between the public wisdom as represented by the recommendations of a citizen deliberative council and the public will as represented by votes and public opinion polls on the same issue raise important questions. Among other things, they highlight the need for journalists, activists, and other storytellers and political players to engage the entire public with the public wisdom being generated by a deliberative mini-public. That involvement would ideally take place before, during, and after the actual citizen deliberative council's deliberations.

There have been experiments with "televote" audiences, large groups of citizens who watch citizen deliberations on television or online and periodically engage with the citizen deliberators by phone or online, providing feedback during the deliberative process. Since the public owns the airwaves at the local level and broadcasters must serve the public interest, communities can and should work with them to present citizen deliberations on issues vital to the community. Another variation involves open-participation public deliberations and debates carried on online before or during the face-to-face ones occurring in the citizen deliberative councils, with some crossovers between the two conversations. In an Australian initiative, members of the larger random pool from which the citizen deliberators were selected were invited to participate in online collaborative work to create the deliberators' agenda. Nowadays, official participants in citizen deliberative councils could also use blogs, chats, tweets, live conference calls, or other technologies to engage citizen observers as ad hoc participants or to engage the public with their council's concluding recommendations. You will find more thoughts about public engagement in chapter 8.

Given their potential to generate public wisdom, how should citizen deliberative councils be used in our public life?

CHAPTER 7

How Citizen Deliberative Councils Could and Should Be Used

It is now well demonstrated that with this method ordinary citizens have a remarkable capacity to grapple with complex problems and come up with useful recommendations that serve the common good, thus realizing the elusive dream of democracy more fully than ever before.

Yet most citizen deliberative councils have only been convened as isolated events or sophisticated focus groups by organizations or agencies seeking input from the public. Only rarely—as in the examples from British Columbia and Denmark described in the previous chapter—are they given any real power in the political process. And only rarely do practitioners, activists, or political theoreticians and visionaries explore the many diverse facets of our public lives to which these citizen panels could be applied. The one pioneering exception is communication professor John Gastil's *By Popular Demand,* from which a number of the ideas in this chapter were taken.

The purpose of part 2 of this book is to show how valuable citizen deliberative councils could be and why it is worth promoting and empowering them—and protecting them, as discussed in chapter 14. Once we see the wide applicability of this approach to generating public wisdom—an applicability almost as broad as the familiar democratic practice of voting—the larger vision of empowered public wisdom and its potential for salvaging our democracy and our world become compellingly clear.

Citizen deliberative councils (CDCs) could and should play many roles to help us take into account what needs to be taken into account in our public decision making. Here are some examples:

Providing Periodic Citizen-Based "State of the Union" Declarations

As embodied by Wisdom Councils and the *Maclean's* initiative, microcosms of the public can consider how things are going in their community or country and articulate the frustrations, concerns, and hopes of the population on a regular basis. They can instigate a "time out" for a community to reflect on where it is and where it is headed, and to creatively tease out new directions and options. Such councils would tend to have more or less open-ended conversations. If the randomly selected participants were given tasks to do in such councils, they would tend to involve the exploration of values, visions, and scenarios more than studying facts and existing proposals. No experts would be needed except for the citizens themselves—who are, after all, experts in their own experience and longings. They could recommend solutions, new directions, or the use of other CDCs to tackle specific public issues. They embody the unconstrained voice of We the People and provide an evocative mirror for the whole population, rather than the highly politicized annual State of the Union address of elected presidents. The regular use of citizen-based "state of the union" addresses would tend to build a strong sense of We the People consciousness in the population as a whole.

Studying Issues on Behalf of the Public and Public Officials

After studying balanced briefings and cross-examining a diverse spectrum of experts, randomly selected CDC members could provide voters and decision-makers with informed guidance about an issue, grounded in the core values of their community. Legitimate issue-oriented CDCs could be convened by legislatures, citizen petitions, prior CDCs, or by other means established by law or popular acclaim, when and as needed. They could address issues broadly, identifying new possibilities—or they could choose from a given set of options (in which case critical attention would have to be given to how those options are chosen and by whom). Annual CDCs could be convened in specified issue areas—such as economic policy, the environment, education, defense, or welfare—to provide an ongoing sense of the best "general interest" thinking in each of these areas. Such annual issue dialogues could be set up such that the CDCs conferred with hundreds of their fellow citizens in the random "jury pools" from which they were selected, in televised or online forums viewable by all—a process that would be educational for everyone, especially if the citizenry was engaged in other forms of grassroots dialogue and deliberation around these issues as part of the same participatory effort.

Reviewing Proposed Ballot Initiatives and Referenda

The randomly selected members of a CDC could interview both advocates and opponents of specific ballot measures, and then share with their fellow voters (through official voters' pamphlets, the internet, and the media) their conclusions about the facts of the matter and their best judgment about the merits of those initiatives or referenda. Such a Citizens' Initiative Review (CIR) could be put in place by a ballot initiative or by legislation establishing a governmental or nongovernmental office to convene CDCs in a timely way to review either all or just certain kinds of qualified initiatives. This would significantly reduce both the special-interest manipulation and the mass thoughtlessness that has recently beset the initiative process, thus cleaning up and revitalizing what should be one of our best tools for popular empowerment. A CIR was officially established in Oregon in 2011. It and a proposal for a national initiative process in the United States will be covered further in chapter 11.

Creating Proposed Ballot Initiatives to Deal with Identified Issues

It is one thing for a CDC to review initiatives created by a special-interest group or legislature. It is quite something else for a CDC to generate initiatives that can then be placed on the ballot, as was done by the British Columbia Citizens' Assembly on Electoral Reform. A CDC would draft one or more versions of an initiative to address a particular issue and interview partisans for their critiques and recommendations until they decided what would be best. Then they would have lawyers or legislators on hand to legally draft the initiative in a form that could be voted on and, if approved, passed directly into law. In a political system more fully guided by public wisdom, a Wisdom Council might identify and prioritize an issue on behalf of the community and recommend that a Citizens Jury or other CDC be convened to make recommendations on it. The Citizens Jury might sketch out policy guidelines they thought would best address the issue. Then an initiative-creating CDC could craft the initiative and submit it for a popular vote. In subsequent promotion of that ballot initiative, advocates could point out that it wasn't created by a partisan interest group but by a group of randomly selected ordinary citizens convened to look into the issue, who became informed about it and used common sense to figure out how it should be handled. Perhaps even better would be to hold several CDCs like this and, if their recommendations differed, to hold a CIR (perhaps made up of members from the preceding CDCs) to recommend which one (or some integration of them) should be put on the ballot. As noted earlier, there is precedent for this: In ancient Athens, a deliberative council of five hundred—the *boule,* whose members were chosen by lot—set the agenda for the community's assembly where everyone voted on the proposals the council put before them.

Ensuring Sober Public Evaluation of Controversial Legislation

Laws could be passed mandating suspension of decisions on controversial legislation whenever a certain large number of people petitioned to suspend the legislation pending review by a CDC. A group of perhaps a dozen citizens might then be drawn from a regular jury pool and given twenty-four hours to hear arguments from both advocates and opponents of the legislation and to decide by majority (or supermajority) vote whether to lift or sustain the suspension. If they decide to lift the suspension, then the legislators could proceed with their vote. However, if the initial jury sustains the suspension, then a full CDC would have to be convened to study the legislation in detail and cross-examine expert advocates and opponents. After the CDC's findings are broadly publicized, the legislators could then proceed with their vote under the watchful eyes of their now better-informed constituents.

Reviewing Candidates
for Elected Public Office

I have seen three interrelated approaches recommended for reviewing candidates—issue-centered, qualification-centered, and interview-centered—each of which is described here.

Issue-centered evaluation

Issue-centered evaluation would involve a CDC evaluating candidates' positions on key issues (perhaps compared to positions favored by prior CDCs on those issues, such as by the "annual issue dialogues" mentioned above, or by the CDCs evaluating key pieces of legislation as described below). For example, before a national legislative election four issue-centered CDCs could be convened to evaluate each candidate in depth on the economy, the environment, security, and education. These CDCs would review the candidates' records and interview the candidates directly, along with their supporters and their detractors. (Three of these were conducted by the Jefferson Center and the results widely reported by the media.)

Qualification-centered evaluation

Qualification-centered CDCs would ask experts and the candidates themselves what criteria should be used to evaluate candidates for the particular position they seek to win. Once the CDC chooses its criteria from that advice, it would have the candidates discuss their own and each others' qualifications in terms of those criteria. Partisan and nonpartisan experts could also testify on candidates' qualifications.

Interview-centered evaluation

Although interviews would usually be part of all CDCs evaluating candidates, interview-centered CDCs would more deeply engage with the candidates, not limiting themselves to positions and qualifications but reaching into each candidate's character, responsiveness to the public, management style, and even indefinable "gut feelings." Having each candidate face various challengers or challenging scenarios for several hours in the unscripted presence of a randomly selected citizen panel could be very revealing.

As previously mentioned, the evaluations of the CDC would be made available to the voters through the media, the internet, and official voters' pamphlets.

An intriguing variant for evaluating legislative candidates (proposed by John Gastil) envisions a CDC convened to pick what the people feel are the ten most important bills proposed or voted on since the last election. Legislative candidates would be required to state their views on each of these pieces of legislation. The voting records of incumbents would already be available on bills that were passed or defeated. Then full CDCs would review each piece of legislation in the same manner that they might review a ballot measure. If a supermajority (67 percent or more) of their members supported or opposed a piece of legislation, their judgment would be recorded as the "people's preference." The percentage of times a candidate's record or position aligned with this "people's preference" would be published as noted above, along with the CDC's and candidates' explanations of their views.

These ratings would be much like the ratings published by partisan organizations like the National Rifle Association or the Sierra Club to approve or disapprove of representatives and senators, except that the CDC ratings would be from a nonpartisan perspective rather than from a particular special-interest perspective. The CDC's rating (say, 20 percent—or 90 percent—agreement with the "people's preference") would not tell voters how to vote. Rather, it would provide a useful "rule of thumb" to augment the guidelines most people use—such as party affiliation, last name, gender, and interest-group recommendations. A further (and controversial) option would be to list the candidates and their "people's preference" ratings right on the ballot in descending order.

Reviewing Government Budgets

Effective review of a government budget would probably best be done by several CDCs. One could review the budget proposed by the chief executive (mayor, governor, or president). Another could review the version submitted by the legislative budget committee. Other CDCs might review the budgets of past years, or budgets proposed by various interest groups, to suggest more general citizen guidelines for budgeting, or to review the effectiveness of past budgeting efforts.

Interestingly, when citizens are allowed to deliberate in an informed way about budgetary matters, they tend to support higher taxes to cover services they believe necessary for a healthy community or country, rather than cutting taxes to have more money for themselves. This fact could have a profound impact on budgetary crises at all levels of government, if there is a citizens' movement to empower informed citizen deliberations like CDCs to evaluate budget proposals and publicize their public judgment to counter special-interest manipulation.

Note that this approach is different from the increasingly popular participatory budget approach used in hundreds of cities worldwide (see appendix 1). A mass-participation participatory budget program is not a randomly selected CDC, but the two could be used productively together.

Reviewing Government or Corporate Performance

Using the same model of hearing testimony from all sides of an issue, a CDC could hear witnesses critique and defend the performance of a public official, public agency, or corporation. This would be a particularly useful tool in touchy areas, such as periodic citizen review of corporate charters, police behavior, or the treatment of whistleblowers. Systems could be set up whereby a certain level of public petition would automatically trigger a CDC to investigate. In all cases, such a system of highly informed and impartial answerability could greatly increase the quality and responsiveness of all forms of power exercised over our collective life.

Summary

The broad citizenry could, if it chose, ensure that its long-term general interests were well and dependably championed through the use of randomly selected citizen deliberative councils. The quality of deliberation involved could replace or shape public opinion polls as an indicator of the public will and the general welfare—especially on controversial or high priority issues. The randomness, brief existence, and possibly even the sequestration of CDCs could make them at least as resistant to manipulation as trial juries. Well-monitored facilitation and briefings could help them produce sophisticated, common-sense results. The fact that they would be rooted in community values could counterbalance the greed, hunger for power, partisanship, and shortsightedness rampant in both public and private sector decision making.

CDCs are flexible enough to evaluate issues, proposals, legislation, candidates, public officials, and the general state of the community. In each case, the kind and quality of information, perspective, and guidance produced by a CDC is unique—and uniquely valuable.

Implicit in this vision is the realization that nowhere

else do we have a trustworthy source of generally accessible public judgment and public wisdom arising from extended high-quality investigation by diverse ordinary citizens deliberating together away from the shallow, one-sided manipulations of special interests.

Whatever issues, candidates, or proposals most excite our passion, they must pass through the decision-making processes that are built into our systems of politics and government. It behooves us to ask: are these processes set up to make sensible decisions on behalf of the long-term common good? If not, we have CDCs as a tool to inject public wisdom and popular will into that decision making. We can give that collective wisdom and will as much power as we choose.

These reforms should start at local or state levels (e.g., evaluating local issues and mayoral or gubernatorial candidates) before they are pushed at national levels (e.g., evaluating national issues and presidential or congressional candidates). However, public servants at any level (including the national) could always convene CDCs to advise them or their agencies—or to influence their fellow public servants, other institutions (such as corporations), or the public at large toward more wisely democratic policies and behaviors.

Underlying all these details about citizen deliberative councils is a larger purpose: to bring about the urgently needed next step in the evolution of democracy itself. It is desirable and likely that regular use of CDCs can help transform We the People from a patriotic myth to a highly conscious and intelligently coherent political force. It can help bring real vitality to the ultimate democratic authority—the people—that is currently fragmented, enthralled, stupefied, and unable to act clearly and consistently on its own behalf.

The revolution in decision making that citizen deliberative councils offer us is of comparable magnitude to the revolution in decision making created centuries ago by the idea of majority vote. It can be applied virtually anywhere, and it could make all the difference in the world.

CHAPTER 8

Public Empowerment, Public Engagement, and the Role of Journalism

It's one thing to be able to generate public wisdom in all the ways described so far. It is another thing to have that wisdom actually impact society, especially influencing public policy. So how do we use citizen deliberative councils strategically to empower public wisdom? What can we do to make such councils part of our usual political process? Here are a few ideas:

Convene processes like Wisdom Councils to evoke the public's awareness of their collective wisdom and power as We the People. This can be done by official proclamation or legislation—or unofficially, simply by grassroots initiative, with no permission from anybody. The Wisdom Council process, which has been undertaken in a number of communities in North America and Europe, establishes a presence for an inclusive, unconstrained, publicly wise "people's voice" in a community every three to twelve months. This ongoing process creates a dynamic tension between what that voice says and the statements and actions of other political players—from public officials to corporations to activists to politically inactive citizens. Over time, this tension draws the population into greater political involvement and pressures all political players into greater alignment with the public good. See chapter 10.

Organize public campaigns to demand that public wisdom processes be given official or unofficial advisory roles in government decision making. For example, Denmark's parliament occasionally convenes Consensus Conferences to gain the public's informed advice on controversial technical issues. Such an advisory role does not interfere with the prerogatives and powers of public officials, but it does create a context that influences their behavior. We can also solicit pledges from politicians stating that they will take seriously the recommendations from a properly convened citizen deliberative council—that is, they will either do what it says or publicly explain why they can't or won't. An example of such a pledge can be found at www.co-intelligence.org/PoliticiansPledge.html.

Convene public wisdom processes to advise voters on issues and/or candidates—and actively publicize their recommendations. Oregon's official Citizens' Initiative Review process uses a citizen deliberative council to review ballot initiatives and referenda on behalf of the voters. It is privately run and financed, but the process is transparent and the results are officially printed in voter information pamphlets. Similarly, the British Columbia Citizens' Assembly on Electoral Reform developed proposals that were submitted to the voters. A number of unofficial citizen deliberations have had an impact on elections, including a Citizens Jury convened by the Jefferson Center that interviewed candidates for governor of Minnesota and for U.S. senator in

Pennsylvania. (The IRS threatened the Jefferson Center with loss of nonprofit tax status if they convened more Citizens Juries on candidates, so they didn't.) As noted in the previous chapter, citizen deliberative councils have been proposed for institutionalized evaluation of all legislation and candidates. And a citizen deliberative council process is included in the national ballot initiative proposal described in chapter 11.

Create a lobbying network or political party specifically dedicated to pushing the policy recommendations generated through public wisdom processes. This has not yet happened, but there are precursors showing up in some parts of the transpartisan movement, bringing people from the Left and the Right together and then promoting what they come up with. See chapter 9.

Create nonpartisan political organizing websites that help citizens find others who share their passion on specific policy options. Help people build alliances and lobbying capacity and generate political power both inside and outside traditional political parties. Then use that system to mobilize and lobby around policy options recommended by public wisdom processes. See chapter 12.

Convene public wisdom processes and promote their findings to advocacy groups who already favor the policies the wisdom process recommends. The advocacy groups could then brag that a group of randomly selected ordinary citizens who carefully considered all aspects of the issue ended up supporting the advocacy groups' position. This might be even more powerful than advocacy groups' current practice of quoting favorable public opinion polls. In doing so, the advocacy groups would champion the public's wise recommendations while simultaneously (intentionally or not) promoting public awareness of the process that generated those recommendations.

Build an alliance of issue-oriented groups who have concluded that their pet issues won't get far without changing the decision-making machinery that decides policy on all issues. They would use part of their resources to support empowered public wisdom initiatives like those in this list.

Create internet-based systems that enable grassroots activists to affordably self-organize public wisdom processes on whatever issues they or their community are working on, whenever they need to or want to. In this way public wisdom processes could become familiar and powerful through widespread use. This option is still visionary, but the capacity to realize it is beginning to emerge. See chapter 12.

Promote the establishment of a fourth branch of government that functions through the deliberations of randomly selected citizen panels. This fourth branch would have power comparable to that of the other three branches, including the power to make laws and approve or disapprove the laws and regulations created by the other branches. This has not been done in modern times, but a number of detailed proposals exist. See chapter 13.

There are undoubtedly other approaches. The point here is that we can use the fact that hundreds of citizen councils have already generated public wisdom to transform the dysfunctional, manipulated, toxic, and quasi-democratic decision-making processes that exist at all levels of society. The ideas above demonstrate numerous ways we can give public wisdom processes real power in our political system. The sooner we do it, the better our chances of making it through the coming political and economic storms and being on track for a far better world than we have right now.

Journalists and Other Storytellers

This cannot, of course, be done without considerable public awareness and engagement—before, during, and after initiatives like these are undertaken. Key to such engagement is the inspired involvement of activists, philanthropists, social networkers, and the many storytellers of our society.

I want to focus here on the storytellers: writers, musicians, moviemakers, artists, actors, media pundits, public-relations people, politicians, and teachers. The most important storytellers of all, I believe—at least for this purpose—are journalists. I'm referring not just to professional mainstream journalists but to bloggers and anyone else who tells public stories about public actions, processes, and issues in our communities, states, and nation. All these folks have major roles to play in birthing, sustaining, and promoting empowered public wisdom.

The success of this probably requires a major partnership between, on the one hand, the organizers and facilitators of public wisdom–generating conversations and, on the other hand, journalists and other storytellers. By promoting public wisdom–generating conversations among diverse people, this collaboration could enable communities to cocreate their own stories of what is happening to them now and how they are going to shape their future.

The journalists' role would be vital at every stage. Ideally, thanks to journalists, everyone in a community would know about any public wisdom–generating conversation before, during, and after it happened. They would know why it was happening and what it was about. They would know who was participating—perhaps they would even attend an event at which future participants were selected with some fanfare. They would have been invited to preparatory and follow-up public conversations—such as World Cafés, Conversation Cafés, study circles, Open Space conferences, and online forums. They would know what the experience was like for participants in all these events because those participants would be interviewed by the media. They would know the results and have forums in which to say what they thought about it all. They would know if and how the recommendations were followed, who was involved, and what the successes and failures were.

This is an expanded version of the traditional journalistic role of empowering democratic citizens with information. Public wisdom–generating processes are extremely empowering to citizens and whole communities. The stories of participants make great human-interest features. The events themselves are dramatic, because heat is generated when we have diverse, ordinary people coming together to discuss hot issues. News outlets love conflict. But deliberative conflict is different from the usual conflicts that preoccupy the mainstream news media. Hot conflicts that evolve into creative solutions are very different from hot conflicts that are chronic, suppressed, or violent. Journalists can show citizens what a profound difference working together can make in our politics. This is not because they are biased but simply because they objectively report instances where people actually work well together on important national and community issues.

We have a supreme example of this type of reporting in the previously mentioned "People's Verdict" experiment done by *Maclean's.*

Maclean's devoted forty pages to describing their remarkable initiative in their July 1, 1991, issue. (Imagine *Time* magazine devoting forty pages of a single issue to anything!) PDFs of the full coverage are available online at www.co-intelligence.org/S-Canadaadvrsariesdream.html. I see those forty pages as a journalistic breakthrough of tremendous importance. They devoted half a page to each of the dozen citizen panelists, including a picture, so that readers could pick whom they identified with and whom they thought was an "enemy." They then provided twelve pages covering the actual conversation—a day-by-day, hour-by-hour, blow-by-blow account of the conflicts and the ultimate healing and collaboration—including pictures of every step of the way, from arms folded in opposition to former antagonists hugging. Other articles in the issue described the process of participant selection, the facilitation method used, and background about the issues that were discussed. The group's final agreement was printed on pages colored like old parchment, with the signatures of all the deliberators at the bottom of the last page, like those of John Hancock and other Founding Fathers at the bottom of the U.S. Declaration of Independence.

Robert Marshall, *Maclean's* assistant managing editor, noted that past efforts—a parliamentary committee, a governmental consultative initiative, and a Can$27 million Citizens' Forum on Canada's Future—had all failed to create real dialogue among citizens about constructive solutions, even though those efforts involved four hundred thousand Canadians in focus groups, phone calls, and mail-in reporting. "The experience of the *Maclean's* forum indicates that if a national dialogue ever does take place, it would be an extremely productive process."

What followed the publication of the *Maclean's* "People's Verdict" issue and the hour-long CTV documentary was month after month of exactly that—spontaneous national dialogue and forums across Canada organized by schools, churches, and many other groups. Citizens had energy to actually heal the country and confront the country's issues together. But then the prime minister was "hammered" in a few of the forums and accused the Canadian Broadcasting Corporation of fixing questions to make him look bad. He became a critic of the process, suspecting impure political motives by the process's advocates. In the end, political agendas and personalities held sway, maintained their business-as-usual patterns, and the country as a whole returned to politics as usual.

Notice the several varieties of public participation we see here. We see the wisdom-generating *archetypal participation* of diverse voices in the mini-public convened through wise selection of typical participants. We see an often transformational *vicarious participation* of the broad public witnessing the deliberations among people they identify with and people they see as opponents unfolding in the mass media. And we see the *direct mass participation* in spontaneous and organized dialogues around the country. Another form of participation not present in the *Maclean's* case, but present in other initiatives, might be called *crowdsourced participation,* in which hundreds or thousands of individuals offer their input, usually online.

In the midst of this appreciation, I want to focus for a moment on the biggest thing that was missing from the *Maclean's* initiative: *iteration.* Imagine what would have happened in Canada if *Maclean's* had done this same exercise again the following year. And the next year. And the next. Imagine that it had also reported on all the subsequent conversations, conflicts, citizen engagements, and activism that came out of those exercises. Talk about a catalyst! Nothing in such a repetitive exercise would violate objectivity or principled news reporting. But it would be a profound expansion of journalism's primary function of promoting an informed citizenry and responsible, answerable leadership in an engaged democracy.

Versions of this could be done in any community, as well as at state and national levels. All it would take is journalists stepping into this new story of a more potent role for democratic journalism.

Citizen deliberations can produce excellent results—real public wisdom. But most of the public, if they have not been through those deliberations, can remain oblivious to that wisdom, or even can be swayed by well-financed public relations attacks into opposing it. Here again, the role of journalists and other storytellers—including public interest public relations professionals—is essential. They can help the public understand what went into the formation of that wisdom (as was done by *Maclean's*) and can help increase general public respect for and attention to well-designed and accomplished citizen deliberations.

Now let's turn to the political environment within which these possibilities exist—and some visionary proposals that could be pursued to launch empowered public wisdom nationally in a big way. Every one of them could be catalyzed and reported on by journalists.

CHAPTER 9

Polarization, Transpartisanship, and Public Wisdom

As this is being written, American politics is, on the surface, pretty thoroughly partisan, very raw, and divided—even the motto of the Occupy movement, "We are the 99 percent," is rooted in opposition to the remaining 1 percent. Meanwhile, behind the scenes, certain power elites are working together to make sure the political culture and government serve their interests, no matter whom we elect. All the divisiveness that apparently exists in our politics doesn't seem to alter the fact that public policy usually and overwhelmingly supports the financial interests of the status-quo economic powers rather than the common good—which is in urgent need of some healthy support right now.

This top-heavy bias in the system naturally evokes populist anger against major power centers—government, corporations, and wealthy elites. Right-wing populism tends to target government, while left-wing populism tends to target wealthy elites and corporations. Both are grounded in a justified suspicion of unanswerable concentrated social power. Both left-wing and right-wing populism are reactions to the same imbalance and have the same basic solution: increase the distribution, answerability, and balance of *all* social power—and, as much as possible, shift power-over to power-with and power-from-within. (See chapter 1.)

The political environment right now is a roiling mix, not only of populism on both the Left and the Right but of people reacting to the extreme partisanship generated by polarized populists. A rapidly increasing political subculture is realizing how much polarization messes up our ability to govern ourselves. They are adding to the long-established nonpartisan efforts of groups like the League of Women Voters and deliberative democracy proponents who advocate balanced political discussions and citizen education about public issues. They seek solutions that address the needs of 80 percent, 99 percent, even 100 percent of the population.

I see eight responses to the polarization of our political culture, some of them newly emerging and some of them long established but recently gaining strength. I list them here in ascending order of what I see as their life-serving transformational potential:

- **Traditional bipartisans**—"Politicians and other powerholders of both major parties need to work better together." This is fine, but "work better together" often means working together to satisfy powerful special interests that run our society, while serving the general public interest only enough to assuage public demands for change. Traditional bipartisans see this as the best way to maintain the basic American way of life.
- **Populist bipartisans**—"Enough of this squabbling and

kowtowing to special interests! Let's get our leaders from both parties to work together to better serve the public good." For example, the No Labels movement.

- **Independents**—"There's too much focus on which party is going to win. I'm not attracted to parties so much as to specific candidates. So I'm going to play the field. I will vote Republican or Democrat or whatever I please."

- **Third parties**—"The two major parties have been taken over by special interests and betrayed us. If we want change, we need to support Third Party X!"—which is either an existing third party—especially the Greens, Libertarians, or the Reform Party—or a new one.

- **Nonpartisan efforts**—"Good citizens are informed, thoughtful voters. Let's provide them with the information and deliberative opportunities they need in order to make informed, thoughtful decisions." For example, the League of Women Voters and VoteSmart.org.

- **Dialogic transpartisans**—"Let's start talking to each other across political boundaries." For example, the Coffee Party and the Public Conversations Project.

- **Strategic and radical transpartisans**—"Partisanship is largely an illusion that traps us into highly generalized and oversimplified opposing camps. We need to get beyond identifying ourselves and each other with Left/Right stereotypes and see each other as complex human beings with unique, nuanced political views and a lot of unrealized common ground. To the extent we can really do this, we will find allies on 'the other side' who—perhaps much to our surprise—support many of the things we support. Different people can support the same things for different reasons. Let's help ourselves, each other, and other people connect and work together to promote the principles and policies we each prefer, regardless of what political parties we or they may belong to or what ideologies we or they may believe in." "I don't care whether you're a Democrat, a Republican, a Green, a Libertarian, or anything else. If you, like me, want to see our country do X, then let's work together on it." Example: the Occupy Together movement and emerging transpartisan advocacy groups (who may be more visible by the time this book is published).

- **Empowered public wisdom advocates**—"We now know that diverse people coming together simply as peer citizens can, with powerful conversational processes and technologies for better collaboration and networking, generate collective wisdom and use it to influence our public affairs. Let's use this fact to generate the public wisdom we need and empower it to improve our communities, our states, our nation, and our world."

I see transpartisan efforts—like Occupy Together participants, who identify with the 100 percent rather than "just" the 99 percent—as preparing the political landscape for intensive cultivation of empowered public wisdom. Partisanship impedes our ability to promote the common good. Part of what I like about citizen deliberative councils and Wisdom Councils and why I see them moving beyond even transpartisanship is that—even when they include political party affiliation as a factor in demographically guided random selection—the deliberating citizens soon set aside the lenses of party and ideology. This allows them not only to see both sides of an issue but also to see important factors and options beyond all "sides." It helps them consider everything that needs to be considered in order to generate long-term broad benefit. In other words, by moving beyond partisanship, citizen deliberative councils help the public be collectively wise.

By publicly demonstrating that partisans can hear each other and work well together, transpartisan efforts help us move beyond the divisive trance of political parties and ideologies and break down those walls. Transpartisanship helps us to start seeing ourselves and each other as members of a community seeking solutions for our community's problems, who collectively hold the power to fulfill our individual and community aspirations.

What we need now is to engage nonpartisans and transpartisans in a movement capable of building the capacity for empowered public wisdom into a major force in public discourse and decision making. I believe future generations will be deeply grateful if we succeed.

Let's look at some visionary proposals to do that.

CHAPTER 10

Wisdom Councils in One Hundred Cities—With World Cafés, Open Space, and Study Circles to Engage the Public with the Results

As you now know, I believe citizen deliberative councils are state-of-the-art methods for generating public wisdom on specific public issues. Below, in appendix 2, I explore research and development activities that could improve them.

Citizen panels like Wisdom Councils and the *Maclean's* initiative, described briefly in previous chapters, have a special—and critical—purpose that sets them apart: They bring We the People to life at a whole-community, whole-society level.

Unlike most citizen deliberative councils, a randomly selected Wisdom Council is not convened to advise leaders or the citizenry on what to do about a specific issue that a convening authority has assigned to them. In both a symbolic and a demographic sense, a Wisdom Council *is* We the People—the ruling sovereign in a democracy—reflecting on what to say to the whole population about the state of the realm. As Jim Rough, creator of Wisdom Councils, loves to point out, "You don't tell We the People what to talk about."

Wisdom Councils constitute and stimulate a collective time-out—a time for reflection, a check-up on how we as a community or society are doing, from the perspective of the ordinary citizenry. Wisdom Councils are designed to be held at regular intervals every three to twelve months (just as elections are held every year or two), and so their proper application is called the Wisdom Council process, since it recurs over and over.

What is a Wisdom Council like? Using Dynamic Facilitation, a facilitator works with the randomly selected participants to discover what concerns they have, what public problems they would like to see addressed (including any creative ideas or solutions they come up with), what visions of possibility excite them, and/or whatever else they wish to explore on behalf of their community. The facilitator is not in charge in the sense of directing the conversation, but rather is the "designated listener," trained to listen to people extremely well and to ensure that he or she understands what each of them is thinking, feeling, and wanting. The facilitator seeks to track and follow the energy of the group—its interests, its passions, its flow, its bursts of insight and creativity diverging and converging as it moves deeper into its challenge—and to record on chart pads the essence of what each person says.

As they feel truly heard, participants open up more, and so do their minds and hearts—and through that opening a fresh creativity begins to flow. They become less pushy or withdrawn and often more emotionally expressive. They become more able to hear each other and to see how things look through each other's eyes, and thus more easily feel and see connections. Meanwhile, as this openness matures, the big sheets of notes collecting on the walls reveal more and more of the complexity and depth of the issues at hand. The spirit of collective exploration and cocreativity intensifies as the group's sense of itself as a coherent, competent citizenship team develops and ripens into a palpable awareness that they *are* We the People. Whatever they choose to say together, from the heart, will be of, by, and for We the People.

At every step, the facilitator looks for meaning and possibility. An outburst, an upset, a conflict from one or more group members brings the facilitator close in, asking "What's your concern?" and really hearing the answer and writing it down. "So what do you think should be done about that?" is the next question, and suddenly the conversation is flowing again, flowing over, under, around, and through all sorts of emerging information, insights, creative solutions, and possibilities. The more it flows, the more the facilitator becomes merely a recorder and occasional summarizer. Whenever it hits a glitch, the facilitator is noticeably present again, freeing up the energy for the group to move ahead to its next understanding or possibility. There are breakthroughs waiting around the next bend and, although the facilitator doesn't know what they are, he or she knows that the group's energy, in its members' search for what will make a real difference in their community, will find those breakthroughs if the conversation just keeps flowing, following the threads of passion and meaning continually emerging in the room.

That's what a dynamically facilitated "choice-creating" conversation is like. It often starts out looking quite disorderly, because participants are pouring out the sundry ideas, feelings, and stories they came in with. Given time—and providing sufficient time is vital for Dynamic Facilitation to work its magic—common concerns, shared perspectives, and new possibilities emerge almost inevitably from the facilitated self-organizing dynamics of the conversation. As in good scientific research, the coherence of what emerges has a special integrity and legitimacy precisely because it came from inquiry, not from imposing prior assumptions on the group from the outside.

The most tangible product of a Wisdom Council is a consensus (or "co-sensed") statement from the group addressed to the larger community or country. No one tells them what to write and there is no form for what it contains. The content emerges as the group attempts to produce it. What the group discovers is, in the end, totally theirs.

The final step in the process involves the group's sharing their statement and experience with the citizenry at an open community gathering (which is, ideally, covered by news media). At one such meeting I attended eight years ago in southern Oregon, the members of the Wisdom Council shared with great animation and amazement that as different as they were, they ended up working well together. They had, indeed, experienced themselves as We the People, and they passionately invited the audience into that role: "We're all We the People. Those folks in the capitol work for *us*. We've dropped the ball on telling them what to do and making sure they do it!" Their revitalized citizenship and power were infectious. The meeting broke up into smaller groups with a Wisdom Council participant in each one, after which people in the audience shared significant insights from their group's conversation. The energy in the room was electric.

Organizers of a Wisdom Council process need to pay particular attention to the relationship between the council and the community, since the whole point is for the process to enhance the community's awareness of itself and its potential wisdom and power. One approach is to have the initial random selection carried out with fanfare in a public way—for example, at a community event or on a local television or radio program—to help build public anticipation and attention. Engagement of media—including local bloggers—is a high priority. The Wisdom Council in southern Oregon was triggered by an interview about Wisdom Councils on a talk show; three separate people in the listening audience called in, inspired to organize one locally.

If you choose to organize one of these, go ahead and engage the Wisdom Council's participants in the community afterward as well. If they'd like, have them interviewed by talk shows, classrooms, or the town council. Put videos of them on YouTube and have them march together in a town parade. The fact that they are "ordinary citizens" inspires and models how anyone can do what they did. Collectively they are not a representative body answerable to anyone, nor do they have any power over any citizen or public official, but they can be a powerful catalyst for a community's dawning awareness of its own wisdom and power.

Remember, though: one Wisdom Council does not a Wisdom Council process make. The process requires iteration. The energy from one Wisdom Council feeds into subsequent ones: citizens called to participate in an upcoming council begin to know—unlike their predecessors—what it is they are being called to participate in. Attendees at one post-Council community meeting get their friends to come to the next one and the crowd grows with each iteration. Each new Wisdom Council group is chosen from a community that has already witnessed and discussed previous Wisdom Councils. With pure random selection, all sorts of people in the community find themselves represented by someone on a Wisdom Council sooner or later. The whole process evolves into greater and greater impact on the consciousness and affairs of the community.

Thanks to Dynamic Facilitation in a Wisdom Council, the public wisdom generated by the diverse citizens' really hearing each other and finally working together is enhanced by the dynamic cocreativity of the process and the level of heartfelt authenticity it evokes in the participants. The resulting consensus statement from the Council tends to arise from a place of deep shared caring and realization.

Given the potential whole-system impact of the Wisdom Council process, I believe it can nourish the growth of empowered public wisdom. Wisdom Councils have been held in a number of locations in North America and, most notably, in Austrian cities and throughout the state of Vorarlberg, Austria, convened by the Office of Future Related Issues (OFRI). In addition, OFRI has sparked Wisdom Councils in Switzerland, Germany, and Lichtenstein, and these, in turn, have stimulated a wave of expanding interest elsewhere in Europe. Many more will have been convened by the time this book is published.

It is time for Wisdom Councils to be used broadly in the United States. We need Wisdom Councils being held at least twice a year in at least a hundred cities and towns for two to three years. We need trained people to organize and facilitate them. There should be a mutual learning community of organizers and facilitators that shares experiences and know-how and debugs and develops the method further, all while publicizing successes among all interested towns and cities. If we do this with intention and support, the spread and success of this innovation beyond the initial hundred towns would be inevitable. It would make a tremendous difference and open the door for many other forms of citizen deliberative council to follow.

Magnifying the Impact

With both issue-oriented citizen deliberative councils and Wisdom Councils—but especially Wisdom Councils—

follow-up public conversations can profoundly enhance the community impact of the council's work. Dozens of methods could be used for this (see appendix 1 for ideas), but I want to feature three in particular. Convening any or all of them to discuss the findings of the original Wisdom Council will draw more of the community into the democratic conversation and emerging public wisdom. Here again, media coverage makes a tremendous difference.

The World Café

This is a simple, powerful process to give participants in a large group many opportunities to speak without anyone getting bored and with everyone benefiting from insights emerging anywhere in the room.

Even though there are endless nuances one can master in hosting World Cafés, they are basically very easy to do, which makes them tremendously attractive for grassroots community work. For all their simplicity, they are very productive and often extremely powerful. All the guidance you need is online at www.theworldcafe.com or in the book *The World Café* by Juanita Brown, David Isaacs, and the World Café Community.

Here's what they're like: the environment is set up like a café, with tables for four. The tabletops are covered by paper tablecloths (often simply a sheet of chart pad paper), flowers, and some colored pens. And, if possible, candles, quiet music, and refreshments are available. Participants at each table engage in a series of conversational rounds lasting from twenty to forty-five minutes exploring one or more questions that are personally meaningful to all of them. In this case, the Café would start by asking people what they thought of the Wisdom Council and its statement. At the end of each round, one person remains at each table as the table host, while the other three travel to different tables.

As the next round starts, table hosts welcome newcomers and share the essence of their table's conversation so far. The newcomers relate any conversational threads that they are carrying from their previous tables—and then the conversation continues, deepening as the round progresses. At the end of the second round, participants return to their original table—or move on to other tables for one or more additional rounds—depending on the design of the Café. In subsequent rounds they may explore a new question or go deeper into the original one. Often the Café host will invite them to look for underlying patterns or new possibilities.

After three or more rounds, the whole group gathers to share and explore emerging themes, insights, and other highlights experienced by individual participants. These are captured on flipcharts or by other means to make the collective intelligence of the whole group visible to everyone so they can reflect on what has been emerging in the room. At this point the Café may end or it may continue for further rounds of conversation.

The role of the Café host is simple: welcome people and introduce the process at the beginning, ring a bell or otherwise indicate the start and end of the rounds, present each round's question(s), and facilitate the period of sharing at the end.

World Café practitioners view the formulation of powerful questions as a fundamental art and skill. Questions for a Café about a Wisdom Council could be, for example: "What could our community do with the Wisdom Council's report that could make a real difference?" and "What did the Wisdom Council miss, and what do we want to do about that?" If you (as planner or host) don't know what question(s) are right for a particular Café, you can ask as a first round question, "What question, if answered, could make the greatest difference to the future of our community?" (For more guidance on creating powerful questions, see www.co-intelligence.org/P-Questions.html.) Engaging together around such questions will give community members a real sense of being cocreators of their community's life—which is the main point of the Wisdom Council.

Open Space Technology

Open Space Technology is a great way for a community to explore all the ramifications of a Wisdom Council's consensus statement and/or organize itself to take action on it. Open Space was created in the mid-1980s by consultant and conference organizer Harrison Owen. He discovered that people attending his conferences loved the coffee breaks more than the formal presentations and plenary sessions. So he created a radically new form of conferencing that has no keynote speakers, no preannounced schedule of workshops, no panel discussions, and no organizational booths. All it has is the passion and responsibility of the participants who care about the topic.

Sitting in a large circle, participants learn in the first twenty to thirty minutes how they are going to create their own conference. Anyone who wants to initiate a discussion or activity writes it down on a large sheet of paper in big letters and then stands up and announces it to the group. Adding a post-it note with a meeting time and place, they tape their sheet to a wall. When everyone who wants to has announced and posted their initial offerings, the whole crowd mills around the wall, putting together their personal schedules for the remainder of the conference. And then it just starts.

Open Space is chaotic, productive, and fun. No one is in control. The whirlwind of activity is guided from within by a handful of simple principles. The most basic is that everyone who comes to an Open Space conference must be passionate about the topic and willing to take some responsibility for creating things out of that passion. One lovely formulation of this by practitioner Peggy Holman is: "Take responsibility for what you love, as an act of service." Four other key principles are: "Whoever comes is the right people," "Whatever happens is the only thing that could have," "Whenever it starts is the right time," and "When it is over it is over."

My favorite Open Space principle is the Law of Two Feet: "If you find yourself in a situation where you aren't learning, contributing, having fun, or otherwise feeling alive, go somewhere else." This includes shifting your awareness or participation right in your present session, as well as the more obvious one of physically moving to another activity. The Law of Two Feet causes some participants to flit from activity to activity: they're valued as *bumblebees,* cross-pollinating ideas. People who go off and sit by themselves are appreciated as *butterflies,* because they create quiet centers of nonaction where stillness, beauty, novelty, or random conversations can show up and add to the vibrancy of the event.

Open Space conferences can be done in one day, but the most powerful go on for two or three days or longer. The longest and best I've experienced were five days long. Participants gather together briefly in the morning and evening to share experiences and announce any new workshops they have concocted. They spend the rest of the day in intense conversation. Even meals are often come-when-you-can affairs that go on for hours, filled with bustling dialogue. After a few days of this, an intense spirit of community usually develops that is all the more remarkable considering that participants are all doing exactly what they want.

If the findings of a Wisdom Council (or other citizen council) suggest actions or shifts needed in the broader community, Open Space is an ideal way to enable people passionate about them to organize together to move things ahead. Open Space conferences are particularly effective when a large, complex operation or situation needs to be thoroughly reconceptualized and reorganized—when the task is just too big and complicated to be sorted out "from the top." Open Space assumes that such a system contains within it the seeds of everything that needs to happen. The process simply provides people with existing passions the opportunity to self-organize into new configurations. For this to work, however, the system's leaders must let go of control so that true self-organization can take place.

Like the World Café, Open Space is basically so simple to facilitate that it can be effectively used by almost anybody. Give it a try with Harrison Owen's *Open Space Technology: A User's Guide.*

Study Circles

Study circles are voluntary, self-organizing adult education groups of five to twenty people who meet briefly three to six times over a period of several weeks to explore a subject, often a critical social issue. In this case, it would be the conclusions of a Wisdom Council or other citizen deliberative council. Each meeting commonly lasts two to three hours and is directed by a moderator whose role is simply to aid a lively but focused dialogue. Between meetings, participants read materials handed out at the end of the last meeting. These materials, compiled by the study circle organizers, are used as springboards for dialogue, not as authoritative conclusions. Groups who want to form a study circle on some common social issue can often get ready-to-use packs from organizations like Everyday Democracy. See www.everyday-democracy.org.

Study circles encourage people to formulate their own ideas about what an issue-oriented citizen deliberative council or Wisdom Council comes up with, and to share them with others. In this way the study circle process helps overcome people's lack of information and feelings of inadequacy in the face of complex problems. Community study circle programs often have dozens of circles running more or less simultaneously and conclude with a large Open Space–like gathering in which community members who participated connect with each other around common interests and plan activities and projects related to the topic of their study circles. As with Open Space, this is a good tool to help the community self-organize around actions related to the citizen council recommendations.

Everyday Democracy provides training materials, study circle packets, and guidance on organizing large-scale and diverse participation in structured dialogue to support and strengthen community change.

Conclusion

Wisdom Councils empower We the People to say it like it is about how things are going in our communities and our country. Other citizen deliberative councils empower the people to come up with real public wisdom on vital issues that concern us all. World Cafés, Open Space conferences, study circles, and other highly participatory conversations engage the broad public to delve deeply into what their peers on these councils have discovered to make our lives and our future better. These processes ground the public wisdom generated by well-designed and facilitated mini-publics in the minds, hearts, and daily activities of the broader public.

This is a radically different, more intelligent, and more productive democratic process than we are used to—a process that produces public wisdom rather than mere public opinion or elite-created policies. To enable it to do its job we need to give all that public engagement and public wisdom real power to make a difference. Let's turn to some ways to make that happen.

CHAPTER 11

Deliberation for Direct Democracy: Citizens' Initiative Reviews and the National Initiative for Democracy

Imagine if we could inject public wisdom directly into policy and law. Imagine if we, the people, could make local, state, and national laws that not only reflected our highest values but also took into consideration everything needed to generate long-term benefits for us and our children's children.

This is where public wisdom meets direct democracy. Done well, this very powerful combination would enable wise rule by the people at last—the venerable dream of democracy—streamlined for modern life and empowered with today's technology. The defining feature of direct democracy is citizens' ability to participate directly—not just through representatives—in deciding public issues, especially by voting on policies and laws. Sometimes the phrase *direct democracy* also carries connotations of face-to-face assemblies and town meetings (as in New England and ancient Athens); of citizen deliberation; of those who will be affected by a decision participating in making it; and of a democratic culture that encourages and enables broad participation through education, child care, time off work, community dialogue, tolerance, civility, and civic celebrations.

In the last decade or so, approaches for online voting have proliferated. As attractive as this seems, I have been wary of this trend for two reasons. First, it can be unjust, in that the results might not be representative of the whole population: many people lack computer or internet access or have trouble with computers and electronic media. This could theoretically be handled by connecting less-wired people to more-wired people, groups, or facilities; by using proxy votes (as described in chapter 2); and/or by weighting votes according to demographics or political perspective such that the results would reflect the proportional views of the community even if the actual participants do not reflect that community profile. These all would help, but they don't quite solve the problem.

My other—and even greater—concern is that so few of these methods include deliberations to thoroughly evaluate the consequences of and alternatives to the proposals that are being voted on. This can make democracy a tool for collective impulsiveness and potentially disastrous collective stupidity. It could bring about the mob rule that elites have feared for centuries, newly empowered with technologies that allow the mob to react en masse, immediately and recklessly.

In many modern democracies the main forms of direct democracy are the referendum—voting on choices presented by the government—and the citizen ballot initiative process—whereby citizens propose a law and gather enough signatures of support to get it on the ballot. The naming, framing, content, and advertising of such a referendum or initiative has a profound impact on how much voters support it. These leverage points provide ample opportunity for manipulation, especially in the absence of adequate public deliberation and campaign finance regulations. In many places where these minimal forms of direct democracy—referendum and initiative—are permitted, the process has become as degraded by special interests as our representative democracy has.

Public wisdom processes can and must play an important role in remedying this—and they are beginning to do so . . . just in time. The most obvious and immediate target for intervention is evaluating the initiatives and referenda themselves. The informed, considered voice of the people—as expressed by citizen deliberative councils—can bring some sanity to the process if it can be mustered and heard amidst the partisan clamor and spin. Here are two approaches to accomplish that.

Citizens' Initiative Review (CIR)

As noted in chapter 7, the Citizens' Initiative Review process is a major step in this direction, and a version became law in Oregon in 2011. Based on the Citizens Jury approach, a group of eighteen to twenty-four randomly selected registered voters is convened and paid for five days to hear from advocates and opponents of an initiative and then to deliberate about it and report their conclusions to the voters. The concluding statement of an Oregon CIR lays out what all members agreed were the facts of the matter, followed by a section clarifying the legitimate reasons one might support or oppose the initiative, followed by how many of the CIR's members supported or opposed it after their deliberations. These findings are printed in the official voters' pamphlet that is distributed to all Oregon voters. Their balanced "Citizens' Statement" stands in stark contrast to the more spin-filled, paid-for partisan declarations in the pamphlet.

This new law was preceded by a trial CIR two years earlier. After two years of work by Healthy Democracy Oregon, in 2009 the Oregon legislature authorized an official CIR pilot for the 2010 election. Two CIRs evaluated two ballot initiatives, with their findings printed in the voters' pamphlet. Surveys showed that 46 percent of the voters were aware of the process and the information in the pamphlet—a percentage that is bound to rise as the process becomes a significant topic of election year conversations and news coverage. The quality and impact of the 2010 CIR process was thoroughly researched before, during, and after the election, under a $218,000 National Science Foundation research grant, which reported the following:

1. *The two CIR panels convened in August 2010 engaged in high-quality deliberation.* The panels conducted a rigorous analysis of the issues and maintained a fair and respectful discussion of the issues throughout the proceedings. The Citizens' Statements included in the voters' pamphlet were thoroughly vetted by

the panelists and were free of any gross factual errors or logical mistakes.

2. *The CIR Citizens' Statements were widely used and helpful to a large percentage of voters.* A majority of Oregon voters who read the Citizens' Statements (65 percent of Measure 73 voters and 57 percent of Measure 74 voters) found the Statements to be helpful and gained new information or arguments; those voters who read the Statements became more knowledgeable about the measures. Voters reported spending considerably more time reading the Citizens' Statements compared to other parts of the voters' pamphlet. Voters who carefully read the Citizens' Statements were much less likely to support [both measures]. The net result was narrowing the margin of passage for Measure 73 and increasing the opposition to Measure 74 from a small to a larger majority of voters.*

The CIR panel strongly opposed Measure 73 and supported 74 by a narrow margin with many concerns. Interestingly, the fact that the voters ended up voting the opposite of the panelists became a point in favor of the process, in the eyes of legislators who passed the process into law in 2011. They liked the fact that it informed and influenced but did not determine voter behavior.

---

*John Gastil and Katie Knobloch, "Summary Evaluation of the 2010 Oregon Citizens' Initiative Review" (Department of Communication, University of Washington, Seattle, WA, January 26, 2010). http://tinyurl.com/coleelc

As of this writing, leaders in other states that have an initiative process—like Washington, California, Idaho, and Colorado—have expressed interest. Making CIR a standard and expected part of all initiative processes is a vital part of institutionalizing empowered public wisdom. This will require funding for carrying out CIRs in Oregon because the cash-strapped Oregon legislature left CIR funding to the Healthy Democracy Fund (www .healthydemocracyfund.org), a nonprofit sister organization of Healthy Democracy Oregon. Funds are also needed to support campaigns to ensure that Oregon CIRs ultimately become state funded, as well as to establish CIRs in other states.

Also, as noted in chapter 7, another initiative-related opportunity for public wisdom is the creation of initiatives in the first place. CIRs are necessary in our current system largely because those who create ballot initiatives are either sloppy in their work (as was the case in Measure 74, above) or are designing them to cleverly manipulate the population under the guise of direct democracy. Having ballot initiatives created, instead, by We the People through informed deliberation starts from a totally different place. Ideally, CDC deliberations would result in general guidelines for a ballot initiative on the subject. People familiar with composing ballot initiatives would compose one or two based on those guidelines, and these would be presented back to the CDC for review. This cycle could be repeated several times until a really well-crafted, appealing initiative resulted. A Citizens' Initiative Review–style CDC with new members could also be convened to consider the proposed initiative from a fresh perspective. A process like this would certainly increase both the quality of the initiative that was created and its prospects for success.

National Initiative for Democracy (NI4D)

The National Initiative for Democracy is a campaign initiated by former U.S. senator and U.S. presidential candidate Mike Gravel. It involves a constitutional amendment and a law that together establish a ballot initiative process at the national level in the United States. It proposes a system through which the public can propose solutions to our collective problems, evaluate and qualify those proposals, collectively reflect on them (using public hearings, randomly selected citizen "deliberative committees," public information campaigns, and even an advisory vote by Congress), and then adopt or reject those proposals through a national election.

The NI4D process does not involve a standing body of representatives making decisions, nor does it replace any existing branches of government. The only established body is its proposed Electoral Trust, an elected organization whose sole purpose is to help the public exercise its inherent powers of self-governance.

Gravel proposes to establish this system not through the constitutional protocols designed by our Founders—because he thinks they are thoroughly corrupted—but by the process that the Founders themselves used when they designed and legitimated the U.S. Constitution—a collective act of the sovereign People. On Gravel's website www.vote.org, any registered voter can vote for or against his proposal. With majority approval—a number equal to more than half of those voting in the last election—Gravel will declare the National Initiative approved by the country and start acting on it.

This out-of-the-box proposal represents a more sophisticated form of national direct democracy than I've seen elsewhere—not the least because it includes a thorough review and deliberation for each proposed initiative (a process described in detail in section 3-I of the Democracy Act at www.ni4d.us/en/act). Through the National Initiative's direct democracy process, the public would not only be able to enact its own laws, it could also amend the Constitution, making it into a living document that serves the needs of our changing times.

Talk of amending the Constitution, of course, makes many people nervous—and rightly so. They fear our fundamental principles might be corrupted by the passing fancies of a fickle public or the manipulations of power-hungry special interests and ideologues. While it makes sense to avoid frequent changes in the most fundamental document of our nation, we also need to remember the words of Thomas Jefferson:

Some men look at constitutions with sanctimonious reverence.... They ascribe to the men of the preceding age a wisdom more than human, and suppose what they did to be beyond amendment.... But ... laws and institutions must go hand in hand with the progress of the human mind. As that becomes more developed, more enlightened, as new discoveries are made, new truths disclosed, and manners and opinions change with the change of circumstances, institutions must advance also, and keep pace with the times.... Let us not weakly believe that one generation is not as capable as another of taking care of itself, and of ordering its own affairs.

— Letter to Samuel Kercheval,
Monticello, July 12, 1816*

The National Initiative proposal is definitely about We the People ordering our own affairs.

Gravel does not fit easily into an ideological box. As a businessman, soldier, U.S. senator (Alaska, 1969–1981), and 2008 presidential candidate, Gravel has earned liberal, conservative, and centrist credentials. He is a sort of mainstream radical who knows the underside of politics and loves democracy passionately. Significantly, NI4D allows "only natural persons" to propose or support an initiative—that is, no involvement by corporations, political action committees, or other special-interest groups (see sections 4 and 5 of the Democracy Amendment online at www.ni4d.us/en/amendment).

---

*http://odur.let.rug.nl/~usa/P/tj3/writings/brf/jefl246.htm

Concerns about Gravel's
National Initiative

There are a number of potential problems I see in this initiative, though none rises quite to the level of deal-breaker for me. Gravel and his supporters are not about to change their proposal, if only because it is in the midst of a multi-year voting process, which would be thoroughly disrupted by any change. However, should anyone want to initiate another model, I propose that the following concerns be considered:

The limitations of proposals, per se

The NI4D model is designed to deal with proposed laws in the form of initiatives. In the NI4D process, each potential law starts out as a proposal, rather than as a formal high-quality deliberation about a problem or issue. Although there is ample room to change such a proposal during the NI4D process, grounding everything in a proposal at the beginning intrinsically limits the level of creativity being applied to the issue that the proposal was designed to address. Proposals often shape our thinking in ways that prevent the discovery of "third way" solutions that may be far better. One way to address this might be to require that any person or group (including a Wisdom Council) who wants to see a new law first name the problem they are trying to solve. One or more citizen deliberative councils could then (with adequate support) be convened around that problem, after which any resulting proposals would be submitted to a review process—again using the citizen deliberative council model—which would choose one or more of them to be entered into the National Initiative process.

While NI4D helps good ideas become actual legislation, we also need to design political institutions that will dependably produce good ideas that We the People think are wise—even before they are put to a vote. Although this isn't formally included in Gravel's proposed National Initiative process, fortunately there is nothing in his approach that precludes such a citizens' movement coming up with initiatives to put through the National Initiative process.

Expedience

NI4D seems slow—appropriately slow, given the profound responsibility it entails. However, social, environmental, or technical problems can crop up—or surge into public awareness—very suddenly, and demand rapid handling. What do we do when such an urgent matter needs immediate attention? Do we leave it to the elected legislature to handle, or should some streamlined form of national initiative process be created to deal with such issues in a limited or temporary way until a full initiative process could be completed on that issue? This is an important matter for careful reflection, because both providing for it and ignoring it present potential pitfalls and opportunities for abuse.

Overwhelm

Research shows that few people can hold more than five to seven items in their mind at one time. NI4D could generate hundreds of proposed new laws from creative citizens. But the more proposals there are on the ballot, the less people will pay attention to the specifics of more than a few of them, and the more inclined they would be to simply vote against everything (or to vote according to recommendations of their favorite interest group), rather than exercising informed citizenship. There may be need for a system for establishing priorities, so that not every popular idea ends up on the ballot in the next election. A mix of opinion polling; online voting on national priorities; and ad hoc, randomly selected citizen deliberative councils may help here (for example, by reviewing thirty-seven proposed initiatives to recommend the ten most important).

Special-interest manipulation

While Gravel's design goes to great lengths to impede special-interest manipulation, there are a number of points in the system where moneyed or elite interests might get a foothold. Such Achilles' heels should be actively sought out and dealt with, just as one would actively seek weak points in one's home security system, or as car companies collision-test their new car designs. Here are a few possible points of vulnerability:

- *Electoral Trust:* The Electoral Trust, which oversees the whole process, is an elected body and is thus as subject to special-interest pressures as any other elected body. Would it help if Electoral Trust candidates had to submit to an evaluation by a citizen deliberative council? The CDC would personally interview them and some of their leading supporters and opponents before they qualified for the ballot. (As noted in chapter 5, this was one of the functions of the randomly selected *boule* in ancient Athens.) Qualified, well-supported candidates could also be placed in a pool from which the final members were randomly selected.

■ *Volume of proposals:* This factor was mentioned above as a problem in its own right. But it also gives a foothold for machinations of vested interests who—through individual citizen allies and astroturf groups (false grassroots)—might try to overcrowd the ballot so that citizens no longer have time to deal with the real issues concerned. If successful, this effort might just confuse citizens about certain proposals in a given election—or it might disillusion them with the whole initiative process, as is happening currently in a number of states. The modifications offered above would help.

■ *Qualifying initiatives:* Many initiatives would be qualified through the gathering of signatures. How do we deal with the fact that some initiative campaigns can afford to hire paid signature gatherers, while others have only volunteer signature gatherers? Similarly, with the option of qualifying an initiative through public opinion polls, pre-poll advertising or advocacy can be biased by the financial involvement of certain players.

Again, this could be ameliorated by having a citizen deliberative council evaluate it and by requiring that any sponsored, official, or professional journalistic comment or advertisement about the initiative refer to the CDC evaluation.

- *Administrative sabotage:* Many laws are passed today that are then poorly implemented or enforced by officials (presidents, regulators, law enforcement). Where is the follow-up to ensure that the people's laws are not neglected by a corporate-controlled national administration or other jurisdictions? An annual citizen deliberative council review of initiative implementation would be one approach to this.

- *Urgency:* This, too, was mentioned above as a problem in its own right. If a special process (with less deliberation or participation) is implemented to expedite the handling of urgent matters, it will have to be made secure from efforts by elite interests to frame certain issues as "urgent" in order to reduce oversight—particularly where expeditious action would commit national resources in situations from which it is difficult to withdraw. Presidents often use this kind of initiative to involve the United States in questionable wars that Congress then finds itself supporting out of patriotism. Similar actions have also been used to get fast-track approval of questionable global trade agreements. Again, a citizen deliberative council intervention could reduce this problem.

Summary

Direct democracy is like fire—a powerful force that can be used for the public good if and only if we carefully observe safety precautions, such as high-quality citizen deliberation. Ideally public wisdom processes would be used to generate good proposals; to give voters good information about them; and, once passed, to evaluate how well they are being implemented.

We need to build such systems soon, so that the public's wisdom can bring sanity into our society's decisions as we surf the rising wave of twenty-first-century crises. The stakes are tremendously high and the prospects for positive outcomes tantalizing.

CHAPTER 12

Empowered Public Wisdom Rising from the Grassroots

Although we can generate public wisdom with the proven processes I've described so far, most of them are expensive and laborious to organize. The adoption of public wisdom processes would go much further and faster if they were designed to require less effort and money (for professional services, travel, and accommodations for participants, etc.). So I've wondered: *How can we generate public wisdom right at the grassroots, with people creating that capacity in their communities whenever they want to? Can we get at least 80 percent of the quality of a professionally organized face-to-face citizen deliberative council with far less expense and effort—especially with smart use of the internet?*

There's also the question of empowerment. We can already generate public wisdom, but it usually has little power to shape public affairs. Even the deliberations in the Citizens' Initiative Review and the National Initiative for Democracy involve judging proposals from interest groups rather than from We the People. *How do we set things up so that the public—especially the deliberative public—is the empowered source of wise public policy?*

Finally, there is the prospect of enhancing the wisdom-generating capacity of citizen deliberative councils by using crowdsourcing dynamics to help deliberators take into account more of the facts, arguments, and options that should be taken into account for broad, long-term benefit. *How can we use the broad public to inform and enlighten the mini-publics convened to deliberate on behalf of the common good?*

Is there some form of enhanced, empowered, wise democracy we could start creating right now at the grassroots? Surely, the answer is yes. There are already many innovations developed or being developed that we can use as prototypes or resources to further this vision.

It would help to have some serious funding to develop further innovations that are sufficiently potent and self-organizing, but if they were designed well, they would not require much funding to keep them going. Like many popular online knowledge creation and social networking sites, good design would allow public deliberation and empowerment sites to function well with minimal management. But developing and launching them would require some pretty intense collaboration among activists, funders, process experts, programmers, and webpage designers. This is especially true because anything that would actually do the job needs to be made as potent and resilient as possible before being broadly released, so that it can show up and spread rapidly before efforts to stop or co-opt it can get rolling.

So that's the challenge explored in this chapter: Let us clarify what it would take to create an inexpensive, self-organizing, self-replicating, and viral deliberative and political power-generating system usable by any community, state, province, country, or other population (a) to find its collective judgment or wisdom about any public situation or issue—in other words, to generate an informed, trustworthy, inclusive voice and will of We the People; and (b) to implement that informed public wisdom and will through direct individual and community action and/or pressure on existing institutions and power-holders and/or future institutions designed for such implementation.

To achieve this we will need to combine the wisdom-generating power of high-quality face-to-face dialogue and deliberation with the distributed intelligence, communication, and networking power of the internet and social media. And we'll need to tap the collective intelligence resources of educational institutions, libraries, community groups, and other parts of society, as needed, to serve the above purpose.

Among the system functions for which we need design solutions are the following:

A. How will issues for deliberation be chosen?
B. How will these issues be framed?
C. How will deliberative mini-publics be selected?
D. How will citizen deliberators be brought into this work?
E. What sorts of deliberative process should be used?
F. How will information and expertise about issues be provided for deliberators?

G. How will the deliberators make their final decisions?

H. Who else should be involved in this?

I. How can participants' interest and engagement be sustained?

J. How can the results of these deliberations impact public policy and public life?

K. What sources of organizing energy and structure could support this?

L. What other resources are available to help us think about and organize this?

So let's explore each one of these for deeper understanding and possible approaches. I'll undertake this exploration as if we were planning for the creation of a grassroots People's Voice network whose purpose was to help ordinary people think and work together to create high-quality public policies that would make a difference in the things that matter to them—and then to gather public and official support to get those policies passed and implemented.

I offer this exploration primarily as a stimulus—to provoke not only appreciations and critiques, but also additional approaches and possibilities. I hope it invokes an evolving community of change agents interested in pursuing these questions further both online and in multiday face-to-face conversations.

Some of the sections below offer links to existing resources or approaches to the challenge addressed in that section. Some of those approaches have interesting explanatory videos which I haven't linked to but which you can search for and enjoy on YouTube.

A. How Will Issues for Deliberation Be Chosen?

We need a broadly participatory system whereby issues can be raised, discussed, and prioritized. This would most likely be a site where anyone can post issues and also rate issues that others have posted—perhaps using priority voting like instant runoff voting. It should allow issues to be displayed in a number of ways—for example, most popular, most recent, random—and it should allow searches for particular issues. It would support both individual and group postings—perhaps indicating ones prioritized by transpartisan groups or CDCs because they are likeliest to have the broadest appeal. There would also be a way to engage experts who are monitoring emerging issues about which the public has little awareness (such as technological developments or obscure repercussions of current events) and that could have a profound effect on millions of people. Such issues would also be included in the emerging roster of priorities for deliberation.

B. How Will These Issues Be Framed?

In contrast with framing an issue for *debate*—using metaphors, images and stories to get people to think the way you want them to—framing an issue for *deliberation* involves developing impartial (or multiple-viewpoint) briefing materials that fairly explain at least the mainstream perspectives and proposals on that issue. We want to give deliberators an understanding of the nature of the controversy without limiting their options. A good framing provides extensive information and guidance to help deliberators explore the values underlying various positions, the arguments for and against each position, the evidence for those arguments, the consequences and tradeoffs implied by each choice, the organizations and thought leaders who support various options, and so forth. Ideally a deliberator can see how a reasonable person could support each of the different approaches. Ideally, as well, each issue or proposed approach would have a place where other issues or proposals related to it or impacted by it could be cross-referenced, to take other relevant deliberations into account and to help mitigate against solutions that create problems elsewhere.

Most issue framings present three to five alternative approaches—since providing only two options would invite polarization and more than five could seem overwhelming. However, a good framing often invites participants to move beyond the mainstream perspectives—to cocreate their own alternatives that integrate the best of the various perspectives, or that step totally outside the limitations implicit in all the given perspectives.

In a sense, the goal with issue framing—and the closely related field of argument mapping—is to provide a holistic, inclusive, multiple-viewpoint *story* of the issue. What's going on with this issue? Why are so many people so concerned about it—and fighting over it? The deliberators are implicitly invited to step into the story to create a new chapter in which they—as the wise, sovereign We the People—resolve most of the dramatic tension present in the battles raging in their polarized realm.

Some organizations create briefing booklets and framings for current issues, which can be used by grassroots deliberation groups. But the system we design should also be able to generate its own framings as needed. So ideally, on our imaginary People's Voice website, there would be evolving cocreated, collectively evaluated framings.

Although ideally such a website would enable anyone to participate, there definitely should be participant ratings and exclusions as necessary, as the issues being framed are usually controversial and the site could be readily abused if it were fully open and unmoderated. Since the purpose of framing is to fairly show all perspectives, there is no excuse for abuse; partisans should just put their views in the proper place in the framing. And since the framings should be of use to the average citizen, it should be designed to remain as simple and accessible as possible even if more complex work on it is going on in the background.

As much as I like the idea of open participation, it may prove necessary to restrict some functions to serious, fully answerable participants. There may be levels of increasingly responsible participation and privilege with users moving up the ranks according to the quantity and quality of their participation. People might also join groups or teams who share answerability for responsible participation and collectively qualify for higher editing privileges. The teamwork of such a group could also increase the value of their edits and add a social dimension that might help recruitment and sustained engagement. (I explore this further in notes about "Civic Circles" below in sections D, H, and I.)

Alternatively, organizers could seek particular participants with time or expertise to make special contributions. One source of such framing work might be undergraduates or graduate students who do issue framings as projects or theses. Graduate theses tend to end up hidden away on a shelf somewhere. Framing significant social issues would allow them to actually make a difference with their research right now. There could also be a way for diverse advocacy groups, partisans, and experts to cocreate framings in a moderated collaborative online workspace or wiki, perhaps working in teams, and then transfer their work to the People's Voice site.

In some traditional citizen deliberative councils, an oversight group is usually gathered together, made up of five to ten partisan experts from across the political spectrum on the issue, who together ensure that the materials presented to deliberators are impartial. The work of such oversight groups could be woven into an ongoing process of online framing issues for deliberation.

It would be very valuable to enable users to rate arguments, evidence, references, comments, and authorities for (a) veracity (factual truth), (b) importance (usefulness and relevance), (c) accessibility (ease of comprehension), and (d) popularity (user approval or liking). Where appropriate, the default presentation of these items should be based on an algorithm that integrates all four ratings, while at the same time allowing the user to view a presentation prioritized by any of these rating categories they are interested in at the moment.

One exception: users would not *rate* the different approaches (i.e., policy proposals) for dealing with the issue, but would rather *prioritize* them, choosing no more than perhaps a third of the approaches listed. The aggregated priorities of all viewers would determine which three to five approaches were displayed on the main framing page for that issue. However, when the user first views an issue's framing page and that issue currently has more than five approaches associated with it, they are presented in random order, to prevent past popularity from unduly shaping future popularity. After the user votes, they will then see the top five vote-getters so far. They can change their vote at any time, with the algorithm recalculating accordingly. On subsequent views, they will see both the top five and, on another part of the page, any new proposals that have been developed since their last visit.

Users should be able to rate each other according to the (a) usefulness and (b) dependability of their contributions. They would also have a rating reflecting their level of participation as tracked by the site. We could also have a transpartisan rating indicating "this person helped me see the other side better."

Such ratings help users evaluate the mass of data and identify power users and abusers.

Systems for choosing, framing, and deliberating issues should be set up to allow citizens and public officials to explore local, county, state (or provincial), and national issues. Vertical and horizontal interactivity among them should be enabled. For example, different counties could share work on waste-disposal issues (horizontal), and many state-level issue framings about education could be aggregated for addressing educational policy at the national level (vertical).

I envision all this included in a Deliberapedia—a crowdsourced, wiki-like database of issue framings that could weave together any and all of these resources—as well as the considerable energies of competing advocates in the debate about each issue—into an informational commons of significant value to every citizen and group in the country, whether or not they are part of the broader People's Voice initiative I'm proposing here.

Finally, here are some existing approaches to issue framing (mostly based on some form of argument mapping):

- TruthMapping—www.truthmapping.com
- Multicentric Issue-Based Information System (MctIBIS) —www.ncdd.org/rc/item/6091
- MIT's Deliberatorium—www.cci.mit.edu/klein /deliberatorium.html
- DebateGraph—www.debategraph.org
- Debatepedia—www.debatepedia.org

- bCisiveOnline—www.bcisiveonline.com
- IPA—Issue/Position/Argument—a discussion of underlying principles of issue framing software—www.dkosopedia.com/wiki/Issue/position/argument www.dkosopedia.com/wiki/Open_politics_argument

C. How Will Deliberative Mini-Publics Be Selected?

One of the advantages of face-to-face citizen deliberative councils is that they have rigorous ways of choosing participants to collectively represent the diversity of the community and be resistant to outside manipulation. This gives them a potential legitimacy that is similar to, but more refined than, the selection of trial juries, which also seeks to convene a cross section of the community. However, in citizen deliberative councils, the selection usually involves establishing a pool of randomly selected citizens (from voter rolls, driver's licenses, phone listings, or other broad samplings of citizens) from which people can be selected to reflect their community's demographics (a "stratified sample"), usually by phone interviews and/or mailed surveys. This is done separately for each council convened. This level of rigor is one of the major expenses of convening such citizen councils, so we need alternatives.

Let us imagine that in any local community where our new-style deliberative network is going to be established, People's Voice organizers recruit at least six hundred to one thousand people (or 10 percent of the community, whichever is less) into a pool of citizens who agree to be on call for deliberative service to the community. One strategy is to recruit diverse interest groups, community groups, and religious congregations to recruit their participants for the pool, suggesting that it will help their perspectives be represented in future deliberations. Another strategy is to hold open public conversations on issues and to recruit the participants into the pool. Those recruited would enter their individual demographic information on the site (which would be secure, only visible to themselves and the algorithm that helps build the pool and select the deliberative mini-publics).

When an issue comes up for deliberation, the algorithm selects four to ten groups of five to ten deliberators who collectively represent the diverse demographics of the community. When they are done with their deliberation, they go back into the pool, awaiting another random selection. Any initial investment in organizing them is ameliorated by the fact that the same pool can be reused in different combinations for different deliberations. Organizers would maintain and increase the size and diversity of the pool, regularly recruiting from groups, organizations, and activities that involve demographic types they seek for the pool.

D. How Will Citizen Deliberators Be Brought into This Work?

If people are going to take away time from their busy lives, they must be given a compelling reason for doing so. It must be something of real value to them: a vision, a thrill, a promise. It needs to be clear what they'll need to do and what they'll get in return.

People are motivated by different reasons, and many of these reasons can be called into play in recruiting citizen deliberators. Usually the top motivation is the chance to have a real impact on their community or country. This is the holy grail of citizen engagement. A number of things can inspire confidence that the deliberator will have an impact, such as if the deliberation has a direct line to public officials (especially if those officials are committed to do something specific with the results, or publicly announce why they can't or won't); if the deliberators' findings and recommendations are going to be presented at a community meeting or published in the news media or on a much-used website; or if a grassroots group has pledged to push the results onto the public agenda.

Related to impact is mission—the chance to participate in an effort to make their community or country better, to revitalize democracy and citizenship; to bring some common sense to government decision making; to realize the dream of Washington, Lincoln, and Jefferson; to take responsibility together for self-governance; and to show that it's possible to do the impossible (i.e., for very different people to work together on behalf of their community and children). Different messages would inspire different groups and individuals.

Moving down to the less dramatic motivators, we find simply the opportunity to make a contribution. This is the quiet cousin of impact and mission. People contribute merely by participating, and will be appreciated for that. There are also the rewards of achievement and pride, of actually getting something done that so seldom gets done in public discourse or even the halls of power. Related to this are the social rewards of a positive group experience: getting to know one's neighbors and people different from oneself; having stimulating, respectful conversations; and working together for a good shared goal. Many people value the simple chance to speak up and be heard and understood. Others can be drawn in by a chance to be recognized—to be mentioned in an announcement, get status in an online community, or be given some award or certificate. Financial payment or other reward is also a potent motivator—if resources can be gathered from a sponsor (including local businesses or nonprofits) or from crowdsourced fundraising.

One of the least researched and potentially most compelling reasons to participate in online deliberation is that it is fun. The challenge here is to make online (and phone) deliberation truly engaging for diverse ordinary people who are not geeks, wonks, activists, or academics. Deliberation has a reputation for being serious and intellectual—in short, *weighty*—and many of the existing online resources that support it are dry, heady, and unappealing. So to what extent can deliberation be an exciting game? That's a question well worth exploring with Jane McGonigal (www.janemcgonigal.com) and other social change gamers (or should I say social game changers?).

Another strategy is to have people in small groups from the start. It may be that putting the people in the selection pool into small Civic Circles to socialize and to work on Deliberapedia or other community services together would engage them and habituate them to the online environment while they wait to be picked for a deliberation.

We should only promise what we can deliver. In terms of the impact of an upcoming deliberation, written or recorded promises from officials or groups who will produce the impact are best. In terms of the personal experience as a deliberator, stories and testimonies from previous participants—such as videos from a post-deliberation public meeting or media interview—are one of the most potent ways to interest new prospects. Stories of people who have participated in similar efforts elsewhere can also help.

Finally, some people will need actual support to participate as a deliberator. In face-to-face engagement we face the logistics of food, travel, wheelchair ramps, and other issues. Even in online and phone deliberation support may sometimes be needed. Someone may need help with child care, with using a computer, with understanding the briefing materials, or with translation services. The more diverse the group membership, the more likely someone will need support. To a certain degree, group members can support each other, which helps the group bond. But there is also room here for students, congregations, civic groups, and others to lend a hand to help someone serve their community in this way.

Ideally, with networks of Civic Circles, people who are engaged in other aspects of the deliberative enterprise would naturally be available to help. See sections H and I below for more exploration of ways to motivate and engage people.

E. What Sorts of Deliberative Process Should Be Used?

Most traditional citizen deliberative councils involve twelve to twenty-four deliberators meeting in concentrated dialogue over two to eight days (distributed over one to ten or more weeks, depending on the method) facilitated by professionals. Since the kind of grassroots system we're envisioning here probably cannot match the deliberative quality of this arrangement, we can seek to augment it in various ways using the distributed intelligence potential of the internet.

Online interactions would, of course, include at least chats, forums, and collaborative document work. If at all possible, it would be best to have deliberative groups engage in face-to-face dialogue as well—perhaps at least at the beginning (to get to know each other) and end of deliberations (to publicly announce their results), if not repeatedly. Face-to-face meetings could happen in living rooms, libraries, community halls, schools, churches or temples, or even restaurants.

We might add conference calls to these in-person and online interactions—especially with software that displays participant photos and facilitates taking turns, as well as videoconferencing and Maestro conferencing (which enables breakout group conversations and "hand-raising"—www.maestroconference.com).

By having several groups of five to ten people (somewhat like study circles or Planning Cells) deliberating simultaneously on the same issue (often face-to-face within the group, but each group relatively independent of the others), we can compare outcomes from the various groups. Similarity of outcomes would be powerful evidence that the will of We the People is fairly clear. However, where the outcomes from different groups differ significantly, we can use that diversity to enrich the deliberations by mixing and matching people from the different groups into new groups to seek higher common ground. This can be done in the spirit of the World Café, with people moving to different groups in some preordained or random order, where they would continue their deliberations. After several rounds of such shifting, if a coherent outcome has not appeared (e.g., on a collective wiki page), members of all the groups could meet together for a day-long plenary deliberation, using the best facilitation available. Dynamic Facilitation would be ideal for this.

Volunteer facilitators/moderators for small-group deliberations can be readily trained by keeping the guidelines simple. Here is an example:

- *Focus:* Encourage clarity about the task, mission, or agenda for the group's work together (in general or in a particular meeting or workspace). Help the group attend to the topic or work at hand and not stray too far. Explicitly record any important off-topic items, noting they should be handled later or elsewhere.

- *Speaking/Listening:* In face-to-face meetings, encourage those who talk a lot to say less, and those who don't talk much to speak up. Taking turns helps everyone have a fair chance to speak. Reflecting what you hear someone say helps him or her feel heard.

- *Civility:* Get group agreement to be civil and respectful—unless you are confident you can help the group use heated conflict creatively.

- *Differences:* Use differences to clarify areas of agreement and disagreement, arguments for and against, and so forth. When people try to convince or contradict each other, clarify their concerns and encourage group effort to creatively satisfy those concerns to increase the level of agreement among them and the wisdom of their results. Know that it's okay to simply leave the differences clarified. Never push for mere agreement that leaves bad feelings and a lot of unhandled concerns.

- *Records:* Help the group record what needs to be remembered or shared.

Basic facilitation manuals are available online. Training and support—as well as live workshops—for managing conference calls can be made part of the system as well. It may even be useful to organize volunteer facilitators into local or conference call facilitator support groups that meet regularly to share experiences and tips. Many cities have professional facilitators who could help with facilitation and training, contactable through their professional networks like the National Coalition for Dialogue and Deliberation or grassroots networks like the Occupy Together movement. Experimentation will help us improve facilitation and process techniques for our particular purpose, as well as improving local grassroots facilitation capacity generally.

Some citizen deliberative councils simplify decision making by telling deliberators to choose among (or rate) preordained options, departing from these only where they have broad agreement to do so. While this can reduce the collective intelligence of the outcome, it may be appropriate where fixed alternatives are built in (such as the evaluation of a ballot initiative) or where available facilitators are not up to the challenge of evoking cocreativity out of diversity and conflict.

Finally, there is the question of using online dialogue or collaboration spaces (e.g., wikis, GoogleDocs, or specially created software), either to help the several deliberative groups collaborate (when appropriate) or to allow participation by or commentary from the larger community, at various stages of the process. People familiar with public uses of such online resources can help suggest fruitful lines of experimentation in this realm.

One intriguing model, known in its proprietary form as Synanim, involves a group of six to ten anonymous members, each of whom writes an unsigned one- to two-page proposal about the issue in question. Then they each read all six to ten papers and choose one to revise in light of what all the others said, with no discussion. They then read each other's papers again. This process iterates through several rounds, naturally narrowing down to a consensus or two to three alternative proposals that can be discussed or subject to further iterations, perhaps with a clarifying question or broader participation.

F. How Will Information and Expertise about Issues Be Provided for Deliberators?

As noted above in the discussion of framing (section B), organizers of traditional citizen deliberative councils convene a committee of politically diverse experts to oversee the fairness of the information provided to the citizen panel, including which expert witnesses they interview. In some methods the citizen deliberators have a say in—or actually choose—which experts they interview. Members of the oversight committee can demand inclusion of specific information they favor, but they cannot exclude anyone else's information. To the extent that they collectively ensure representation of a full spectrum of (at least mainstream) viewpoints, they deflect criticism that the process is biased. This is an important factor in *collective intelligence* (which learns from and integrates diverse views), *perceived fairness,* and *democratic legitimacy* (the willingness of ordinary citizens and officials to respect the outcomes of the process).

Unfortunately, most traditional citizen deliberative councils seldom use the internet as an information source and are often weak in including creative perspectives and options that have been developed outside the mainstream discourse on the issue. We could and should change that in our grassroots People's Voice system.

Finally, traditional citizen deliberative councils provide a unique opportunity for citizens to interview and cross-examine experts on the issue they're deliberating. This is a hallmark of the process, and vital to helping deliberating citizens clarify the issue. However, providing stipends and travel costs to expert witnesses can be a major expense.

So three questions come to mind:

1. How do we ensure demonstrably balanced expertise and information for deliberators in a grassroots online process?
2. In addition to the issue-framing systems explored above, how do we use the unprecedented information-gathering capacities of the internet to inform deliberators—even beyond mainstream perspectives?
3. How do we use modern technology to reduce the cost of access to expertise?

Some approaches for each of these:

1. *Balance:* Regarding the first question, organizers could contact advocacy groups on different sides of the issue, asking them whom they would consider to be legitimate experts to oversee such a process. If there were a national or international movement around this—a concerted effort to generate an inclusive, wise People's Voice—lists of willing experts on various sides of various issues could be developed (centrally and/or through the efforts of diverse local groups and/or crowdsourcing) and made available online. These lists could be used to provide experts to oversee information fairness as well as to provide expert witnesses to represent competing perspectives. Cooperating academic institutions may also be willing to provide expert overseers. Explicit approval of an expert by a known partisan advocacy group legitimizes that expert as a representative of a particular part of the spectrum of opinion on that issue—a useful fact when trying to present a balanced group of experts. Names of partisan or neutral authorities could be solicited from the public and embedded in the online framing of issues.

Balanced information would naturally be provided through the online system of crowdsourced issue framing. If the framing covers diverse approaches to the issue, if each approach has arguments for and against it, and if each argument has evidence related to it, that should ultimately generate balanced information. If certain information is missing, deliberators or supporters could research it and enter it into the framing or ask an appropriate partisan group to do that.

2. *Internet as resource.* One way we might harness the internet for citizen deliberative activities is encourage deliberators to use it between meetings—or we might even divide them into teams to see which team can come up with the most interesting information and/or options from the internet within a specified time. Some people may require assistance from their more internet-literate fellow deliberators or volunteer nonpartisan internet research assistants. This internet searching could go on before, during, and/or after other aspects of the group's deliberations. It may be that after they have explored the pros and cons of mainstream proposals, they will be informed enough to understand and evaluate other options. They can then get expert critiques of those new options, back and forth, until they are satisfied that they understand the best solutions available.

3. *Experts:* Deliberators could interview experts by audio and video teleconferencing and conference calls, as well as through email, chats, and various kinds of online forums. Such interactions would be most useful when diverse experts and citizen deliberators can all hear and respond to each other. Body language can be an important factor in judging the information being provided, especially in cross-examination, so video or face-to-face interaction is desirable. We'll need to research what is lost and gained through expert consultations that aren't face-to-face. Obviously, if experts are willing to show up at a face-to-face gathering (which is easier and cheaper if those experts are local), effort should be made to gather all the deliberators

159

together to efficiently engage with them, even if the deliberators deliberate separately afterward.

G. How Will the Deliberators Make Their Final Decisions?

In all, I see several distinct modes of policy selection that could be enabled with the People's Voice system:

1. A formal face-to-face citizen deliberative council
2. A People's Voice version of a citizen deliberative council, mostly online, requiring at least 80 percent support for main recommendations
3. Randomly selected straw polls at the request of public officials or others
4. The overall popular vote of People's Voice network participants for policy solutions that are presented in Deliberapedia
5. The overall People's Voice network vote weighted to reflect the appropriate demographic and/or trans-partisan distribution
6. The vote of power users, who are theoretically more informed

Numbers 1, 2, and 3 need to be specially organized, separate from the general flow of activity in the People's Voice network. Numbers 1 and 2 produce legitimate public wisdom that is worth highlighting in some way on the site and worth lobbying for in the political arena. Number 3 produces aggregates of public opinion from a population that is somewhat better informed than the general population, but it doesn't inherently qualify as public wisdom. Numbers 4, 5, and 6 require little work, are advisory for political players, are of ongoing interest to visitors, and continually evolve as participants and visitors enter and change their votes.

In this section I'll focus mainly on number 2, because what we're looking for here is readily accessible grassroots public wisdom.

During the research phase of this project, we will want to see what level of consensus can be reached by groups that are largely online, while recognizing the limitations of our design for that (i.e., dispersed groups or individuals with nonexpert facilitation). Probably it is most useful to have different levels of agreement being expressed simultaneously on different aspects of the evolving findings and recommendations. Ideally software could facilitate straw votes and sort conclusions by level of agreement, and as deliberation proceeded, conclusions would move up or down the levels and be edited as well.

In the end, different levels of agreement could be reported in the group's final statement. For example, the findings could announce (a) what there was full agreement on; (b) what received 80 percent agreement; (c) what received 67 percent agreement; (d) what received mere majority agreement; and (e) any coherent minority statements (like the minority opinions issued by U.S. Supreme Court justices alongside the majority opinions).

Given the not-so-robust nature of our process, it is

probably best to strongly advocate only for those decisions that are supported by at least a supermajority (two-thirds or more) of the deliberators—and leave the rest to the adversarial partisan battle, rather than claiming it as a legitimate "people's voice." But we should also realize that if groups of a few dozen randomly selected (and thus diverse) people have studied and deliberated on an issue and come to 80 percent or more agreement on a solution, that's a truly remarkable fact that should be recognized as valid public wisdom despite the small sample. It means something radically different from an opinion poll, a single expert's advice, or a politician's position. It is something new and potentially powerful in the political arena.

Another role that could be created in this system would be transpartisan mediators whose specialty is helping strong partisans work out their issues creatively. In addition to people already capable in this work, an algorithm could track and identify participants who propose approaches that generate the fewest concerns and the most support (especially at times when data about who supports what indicates a deep conflict). Similarly, if an issue seems stuck, those with concerns could be called together to work it out. A special part of the website could be reserved for mediating—or scheduling conference-call mediations of—such conflicts, with special rating points given to all those who participate successfully.

The site could track a person's opinions in the context of other people's views (like Amazon's "people who bought this also bought that"). People who want transpartisan engagement could then ask the site to show them positions or arguments that they disagree with, so they can develop and post contributions that seek to bridge the gap between their perspectives and those of the people they disagree with.

Another approach to generating agreements is to include the larger community (the whole city, state, or country—or just the larger community of People's Voice participants) in evaluating proposals from the deliberative groups. If several policy options are presented that are supported by, say, at least 40 percent of the deliberative participants, these options could be submitted to such larger communities for a vote.

In general, the fewer participants and the weaker the process (in design and facilitation), the higher the level of agreement we will need in order to generate a recognizably legitimate people's voice—and this assumes a good diversity of participants, preferably chosen randomly or otherwise embodying the diversity of the community. Most trial juries, which only have twelve people, can be viewed as a legitimate expression of the community because they come to full consensus. With thousands of people and little deliberation—as in a poll or local election—51 percent is considered adequate to represent the "will of the people."

Since our current proposal involves twenty to one hundred citizens and medium-quality deliberation, somewhere between three-quarters majority and full consensus might be considered acceptable as a valid voice of the people—if these people are adequately diverse and the process is demonstrably unbiased. However, research is needed to assess whether the public agrees or could agree to the legitimacy of such a panel, since we're not just going through the motions here. We want to generate a deliberative voice of the people that will be recognized by the vast majority of the population, so that this voice can then be legitimately empowered by their support.

H. Who Else Should Be Involved in This?

The more the public is involved in the deliberative process, the more they will understand what is going on and why, and the more they will "own" and support the results. We've already seen how including too many people in the final deliberations can degrade the quality of the results. But to the extent that we don't engage a lot of people in the whole process, we'll find it much harder to achieve effectively empowered public wisdom. Some of the same principles we explored above for engaging the pool of citizen deliberators can be applied to engaging others, and do not need to be repeated here.

I use the term *Civic Circle* to describe members of the People's Voice network who work in a coherent group over a period of time. I don't have a restrictive definition of what they do in such groups.

Ideally, a large People's Voice network made up of both individual contributors and Civic Circle groups would form the core participants in this public wisdom–generating initiative. Some individuals and Civic Circles would make specific commitments (such as four hours of work a week for two months, to be reconsidered at the end of that time) and get some special status for that—but most would not have made such commitments. Some of them would be members of local, state, and national pools of prospective citizen deliberators, but most would not. Some would be working on Deliberapedia the way the Wikipedia community works on developing and maintaining Wikipedia. A few would be organizers, facilitators, fundraisers, or support people for the special mini-public deliberations. Some would be committed media people. There would be some Civic Circles of artists, videographers, street performers, and other creative people who would create aesthetic, educational, or dramatic works around political issues, which they would tie into Deliberapedia and mini-public deliberations. And so on.

Active people at the core of the People's Voice network could be a vibrant community dedicated to creating and empowering public wisdom in whatever ways they could. Around that core would flow more casual visitors—observers and occasional contributors. All would be engaged by social-networking software enabling them to connect for work or conversation on political issues—as well as general socializing—within and across political divides.

People's Voice network organizers would actively recruit others to participate in online and face-to-face public conversations, to issue priority ratings, and to vote on proposed solutions, and then the organizers would invite the newcomers to become further involved. They could join Civic Circles organized by location (for in-person meetings) and/or by focus (for dialogue or shared work, online or in their local communities).

In some areas the People's Voice network would be used to give input to public officials and politicians willing to work with it. These politicians might ask for survey responses or feedback from partisan or transpartisan Civic Circles on some issue or proposal, or track the progress of online issue framings and expressions of support for various options, or they might sign a Politicians Pledge to take seriously citizen deliberations held by the network. Their engagement would be a key plank in their election platforms.

The startup page of Deliberapedia and the People's Voice network would be clean, easy, and addictive, like Twitter or Google or YouTube. It might include a short video introduction and a few key questions on the visitor's opinions and issue interests. A visitor's answers to those questions would then generate top-layer issue framings (in simple graphic form) for one or two of their top issues, plus links to profiles of a few other people in their local area who hold similar views—and some who hold different views, but who'd like to talk with people of varying opinions. The point is to keep it simple, clear, and focused, with each page inviting engagement that produces the next page deeper into the system or sustains a loop of engagement (e.g., you can't see the overall ratings or answers until you submit your rating or answer).

This would hold the visitor in the site with an attention-absorbing experience. They can then be tempted to do low-level Deliberapedia edits . . . or join issue-focused teams or Civic Circles . . . or post to forums connected to a current citizen deliberative council . . . or sign up for the deliberator pool . . . or . . .

I. How Can Participants' Interest and Engagement Be Sustained?

Not only do we need to attract people out of their busy lives to participate, we need to make this adventure a vital part of their busy lives. All the above, if done well, will encourage people to stay with the program. But what else can we think of to get people enthusiastic about it and stick with it?

In general, I see four main motivations for people to return again and again to an online community activity like this:

1. Passion—values, interest, stake, caring, need, love of the topic, vision, purpose, contest, some action-stimulating emotion (indignation, fear, desire, determination)
2. Rewards—fun, enjoyment, money or other material payoffs, status, influence, success at a challenge, pride, self-improvement
3. Social glue—duty, loyalty, involvement of family and friends, belonging, group expectations, responsibility

for others, answerability systems, communication from a "buddy"

4. Ease—simplicity, elegance, compatibility with other aspects of users' lives, low barriers to entry and persistence, low effort

There are obviously hundreds of ways to apply the above four motivational factors. But I want to highlight several areas that might easily be overlooked in designing such an activity.

Buddies and Teams. The idea behind teams and Civic Circles is to engage the "social glue" factor. I can even imagine that early on there might be a bit of match-making (à la dating sites like OkCupid) between a newcomer and longer-term members who have volunteered to be helpful buddies. Based on profiles and responses to questions, possible buddies are presented to the newcomer, who checks them out, communicates with them, and picks one or a few. The software could also enable volunteer mentors to just show up and offer help and companionship, as happens in Second Life (and sometimes real life). This goes way beyond online support forums and chats and even the old computer users groups. It is a very human connection, intended to be ongoing. Ideally, real friendships would develop out of this and new people would be drawn into social circles where the other dynamics (rewards and passion) would play out individually and collectively (such as competitions between teams working on framing an issue they all care about from different angles).

Resources. Money should be available (a) to support and reward people and teams who are making exceptional contributions to the system, even to the point of providing a livelihood for doing that; (b) to fund citizen deliberative councils in both their online and face-to-face forms; and (c) to fund direct grassroots initiatives—education, promotion, organizing, lobbying, and/or implementation of recommendations arising out of citizen deliberations. Start-up funding may well be through traditional philanthropic lines, but ideally the system would develop its own powerful crowdsourced funding functions, like IndieGoGo and Kickstarter, to the point of even enabling ongoing support for "agents of public wisdom," perhaps through monthly donations like those being innovated by CrewFund.org or being part of an online gifting community like Kindista.org.

Stories. Stories motivate more people more deeply than practically anything else. Ideally, the site would have a section for stories—written, spoken, and videoed. Stories of people's participation in the People's Voice network would encourage participation by others. Stories of how people were personally impacted by an issue or why they are so passionate about an issue or proposal would provide human interest and understanding. News stories and histories of issues and proposals would provide context. Stories from times and places when a particular solution was implemented would provide compelling evidence for or against it, or even inspiration around it. Imaginative scenarios of future possibilities—both positive and negative—and "backcasting" stories looking back from the future could suggest possible initiatives and consequences that should be considered. And of course, stories of public or official conversations that considered an issue or policy—especially where a good collective decision was reached—to provide motivation for us to persist in our own conversations. All these stories could be linked to and from the relevant part of the issue-framing argumentation, but they could also exist as an attractor that brings new people in and keeps existing members engaged to see the latest stories—perhaps even presented in newspaper or blog format, with space for comments and ratings. The most popular stories would rise in visibility and might even be published or broadcast in local or alternative media—the promise of which would invite more storytelling from more people.

Mobile apps. This is part of the "ease" motivation. Can mobile apps be developed to enable people to participate in Deliberapedia and converse with others on some issue for which a decision-maker wants community input? On-the-run participation could increase and sustain greater ongoing participation in all aspects of the system.

But perhaps the most powerful motivating factor would be the guarantee that one's engagement in this exercise of democratic wisdom would have demonstrable and repeated impact on the actual policies of governments and the troubling real-world conditions we've all been living in. That guarantee can be made real for us only by our collective resolve and collaboration. But it can be made.

J. How Can the Results of These Deliberations Impact Public Policy and Public Life?

There are many ways to create impact, among them these:

Dialogue. Promote more conversations on the topic—as explored in chapter 10—with forums in which community members can talk about the deliberators' findings and recommendations as well as hearing the deliberators' personal stories about their experience in the deliberations. In addition to online forums, face-to-face modes like World Cafés, Open Space conferences, and study circles can help ripple the results out into the community, especially if they are seeded with participants from the original deliberation. A community World Café could be kicked off with the deliberators sharing their experiences. Alternatively, a public forum could be held in which relevant public officials join the deliberators for a dialogue in "fishbowl" style (see appendix 1), viewable by the public. Citizen deliberators would explain how they came to their conclusions and the public officials would describe how they see the issue, to the enlightenment of everyone involved, including the viewing public.

Media. The more, and more varied, media coverage of any public deliberation, the better. This includes press releases, media coverage of public events where the participants report their findings and recommendations, media coverage of the "human interest" aspect of the changes participants went through during the process, letters to the editor, talk shows, and so on—as well as online publicity and commentary such as blogs, websites, and chat on Facebook and Twitter. Ideally, in many areas it would be possible to build alliances with media interested in being creative catalysts for building this democratic capacity while generating stories their readers or viewers will love. For an example of truly remarkable mainstream media coverage of a citizen deliberative council, see the story about *Maclean's* magazine in chapter 8.

Lobbying and mobilization. Here is where online phenomena like bloggers, MoveOn.org, MeetUp.com, various crowdsourced marketing and funding sites, and others can be used to empower the public to ensure its collective wisdom is heeded. These could provide innovative ways to spread the word, to craft messages and media, to fundraise, to mobilize demonstrations or community engagement in recommended community projects, to lobby, and to engage people in face-to-face assemblies on behalf of solutions recommended by duly convened citizen deliberations. This need not be a matter of developing new technologies, so much as using state-of-the-art activist organizing and networking technologies on behalf of the whole rather than merely to push a partisan agenda. *That* is a critical shift that would change everything.

An emerging and ambitious online resource, the Interactive Voter Choice System (IVCS) is being designed to enable citizens to organize around policy options they agree with, regardless of what party or ideology they favor (www.reinventdemocracy.net). This would be incredibly valuable to empower the voice of public wisdom, if it were designed to include and feature that voice. While I'm doubtful about IVCS's power and resilience in its current form (as of January 2012), I consider its visionary scope and use of social networking to be a breakthrough. In order to fulfill its mission, I believe it would have to be far more attractive, sticky (so engaging that it is hard to stop using it), and viral (so compelling that people quickly share it with their networks). We would need considerable support for—and participation in—research and development to enable that resource, either through the existing platform or through a new one based on a similar vision.

A similar empowerment effort with a different logic is A Greater U.S. (www.agreater.us), which allows users to propose a bill they would like Congress to pass and the president to sign into law, and to rate the submissions of others in an annual collective effort to define the most important bills the public wants that year. They then collectively pressure politicians to pass a bundle of the most popular bills, using "the greater middle" as the "third force" swing vote in American politics. The bill selection process includes a politically weighted voting system to ensure transpartisan support.

Involvement of politicians and other leaders. Many politicians and public officials can be influenced by what the public—particularly an informed, inclusively deliberative, active public—say and want. One approach is to allow them to view deliberations, participate in them, show up as expert witnesses and/or engage in public forums as described above in the first part of section J: "Dialogue." Their involvement can even be as low-key as the public official's having a private hour-long interview with several of the citizen deliberators, just to get a feel for how the educated public thinks about the issue. Another way is to actively solicit the prior support and/or sponsorship of public officials for such citizen deliberations. They can sign a Politicians Pledge (e.g., www.co-intelligence.org/PoliticiansPledge.html) to take seriously the results of any duly convened citizen deliberation. Several public participation–oriented politicians (especially if they are politically diverse) can sponsor certain citizen deliberations. Their engagement—or lack of it—can be made into a campaign issue to motivate politicians to get more involved in, and even to advocate, citizen deliberations that generate legitimate public wisdom. Similarly, other community leaders can be usefully involved, especially if they represent a broad spectrum of normally adversarial views and/or have extensive networks that may be impacted or activated through the involvement of their leaders.

Cultural embeddedness. This kind of ongoing deliberative process can, over time, become the legitimate, wise voice of the people if, and only if, the majority of citizens come to expect and respect its work. Given a good, supportable, and regularly carried out process, a culture of deliberation will grow such that people will await the results eagerly, refraining from making up their own minds about an issue until they have heard the voice of the people (which does not dictate, but provides information in a unique, useful, and potent way). This sense of expectation can be nurtured by carrying out the initial participant selections (and the other steps of the process) transparently. Once this process has a good record of success, the opening of deliberations and the announcement of results can be done with some fanfare to further engage the public in the proceedings.

Institutionalization. Ultimately, when the process is well developed, proven, and broadly known, it may be embedded in local, state, and national political and government institutions (unless, of course, it has grown to supercede them), as described in chapters 6, 7, and 13. At this point, however, such visions are simply future possibilities. Chances are that this effort will evolve in unpredictable ways, some of which may even make institutionalization irrelevant.

K. What Sources of Organizing Energy and Structure Could Support This?

I suspect that the initial organizing energy for something like the People's Voice needs to come from a small group dedicated to realizing that possibility. Something this complex and embedded in a dynamic system like American politics and technical developments cannot simply be planned out ahead of time and then set in motion. It must be done in a participatory, flexible, and responsive manner, and those involved—especially funders—must realize that such flexibility is necessary and potentially powerful.

When a good beta design is worked out, it can be spread by bloggers, seeded by dedicated teams (for example, as was done by Beyond War in the 1980s, when about a dozen families moved to swing states and catalyzed self-replicating living-room presentations demonstrating that war was obsolete, a meme that thereby spread rapidly). The beta design could also be spread through collaborating organizations. This approach has been used since the early 1970s by National Issues Forums, which provides materials and training for deliberation and promotes those resources and their resulting successes to community groups, churches and temples, nongovernmental organizations, educational institutions, and receptive public officials. And once deliberations are held, chances are good that some of the deliberators will be interested in helping spread the excitement and power they experienced, as long as they get some support for doing so.

An existing alternative political party that shares the goal of listening to and empowering inclusive, informed public wisdom may also be interested—or such a party could be formed to focus on this. A "People's Voice Party," for example, could be dedicated to advocating whatever policies come out of citizen deliberative councils and other well-organized citizen deliberations that met its standards. It would take no positions on issues except where public wisdom processes had clearly articulated what the public wanted, through deliberative dialogue and supermajority agreement or consensus. Other than that, its only position would be to empower the people's voice—both through widespread high-quality public dialogue and deliberation (and high-quality information and technical infrastructure to support it) and the institutionalization of official ad hoc or periodic citizen deliberative councils of various sorts, explicitly empowered to influence official decision making.

L. What Other Resources Are Available to Help Us Think about and Organize This?

There are a number of efforts that, in their own way, reflect this kind of cocreative participatory democratic vision—although not with a focus on public wisdom. I include two here as examples:

Civic Evolution—www.civicevolution.org—An online space to help citizens thoughtfully seek common ground together about desired changes they can make in their community. Using a system for cocreating and rating "curated talking-points" (a good way to chunk deliberative units), teams develop coherent, actionable proposals they can use to garner support from their community and local government, which can be pursued both online and face-to-face.

Democracy Lab—www.democracylab.org—A website dedicated to engaging the public in a merit-based forum for public dialogue and creative problem solving, and for improving communication between public officials and their constituents. It proposes to help people foster connections between their values, their objectives, their favored policies, and the laws implemented by their government.

In closing this chapter, I want to highlight two notes regarding all the websites listed herein:

First, the People's Voice vision I presented here focuses on generating public wisdom about public policy. We also need the capacity to generate empowered public wisdom to guide community self-organization—along the lines of Civic Evolution. It may or may not be possible to combine these two functions in one site while keeping it simple and functional. But this is definitely worth considering.

Second, analyzing and evaluating the gifts and limitations of these innovative approaches are beyond the scope of this book. Suffice it to say that they are quite different from each other, based on different assumptions and providing significantly different ways of exploring and working with an issue, suitable for different groups and uses. What I would hope is that by exploring in detail these and other technologies for issue-related work, a group seeking to pursue the vision of empowered public wisdom would gain valuable lessons for the creation of something that reaches far beyond them all in its simplicity, appeal, functionality, and power to evoke democratic wisdom and transformation.

Now let's turn to the most powerful possible application of public wisdom—an official legislature of ordinary citizens who could both contribute to and use all the grassroots deliberation resources we've just explored.

CHAPTER 13

Citizen Legislature: A New Branch of Government?

I've seen a number of proposals to establish a randomly selected citizen deliberative body as an institutional part of the federal government and possibly state and local governments as well. They fall into two broad categories:

1. *An empowered legislative body made up of randomly selected citizens.* In *A Citizen Legislature,* Ernest Callenbach and Michael Phillips propose an institution designed to replace the House of Representatives. Ethan J. Leib's *Deliberative Democracy in America: A Proposal for a Popular Branch of Government* imagines a fourth branch of government separate from the legislative (House and Senate), administrative, and judicial branches.

2. *Randomly selected pools of citizens to advise the government.* These groups would provide advice on policy matters on request or, perhaps on some issues, automatically. Pollster Steven Kull's Program for Public Consultation envisions a large, established Citizen Advisory Panel or Citizens Cabinet from which citizens can be selected for surveys, deliberative polls, and face-to-face citizen assemblies. Political scientist Robert A. Dahl, in his *Democracy and Its Critics,* envisions convening "minipopuli" consisting "of perhaps a thousand citizens randomly selected"

from the entire population, which could either identify issues that needed deliberation or deliberate on a particular major issue. They would be empowered to "hold hearings, commission research, and engage in debate and discussion," but not necessarily make final decisions.

In this chapter I explore another option based on—but different from—those above. I urge you to critique the proposals I offer while keeping in mind that we need to compare them to the politics and government we have now, rather than comparing them to some unspecified, perhaps unattainable ideal. Every proposal and solution has trade-offs. I've done my best to minimize the inevitable trade-offs in the approaches I describe and advocate in this chapter. But as you imagine these proposals put into practice and find yourself with objections, consider whether your critique also applies to the political and governance systems we have now. For example, if something in my proposals seems unfair or corruptible, compare it to how unfair or corruptible our current system is. If your critique applies to our current system as well, then think about whether the trade-offs in what I propose are acceptable to you, given the considerable benefits. Or perhaps think up some other solution that would avoid the trade-offs you don't like. Be creative. The ideas proposed here are intended to stimulate exactly such creativity.

So now let's consider what a new branch of government based on public wisdom might look like.

The second category described at the start of this chapter, of official citizen deliberative panels that are only advisory and not a sitting body like a legislature, would probably be easier to institute. In particular, it would require no constitutional amendments. It might be a very wise first step, because if it were well designed and facilitated, its activities and ability to generate public wisdom would become well known and more respected by the population at large. After years of operation, more people would start to wonder—given the obvious ability of ordinary citizens in these advisory bodies to generate good policy recommendations—why they aren't given the power to actually make laws themselves. People might then be more receptive to proposals that gave such bodies more power and might support a constitutional amendment campaign that could have been underway during those years.

The issues involved in realizing institutionalized public wisdom at the federal level, a fourth branch of government, are more numerous and complex than can be fully addressed here. I'll describe a few and suggest solutions, realizing full well that different reasonable approaches could be offered for each one of the specifics I explore. Ideally, a series of citizen deliberative councils would be held to explore what approach(es) would best serve our democracy. In the meantime, you might ask yourself: What would *you* do with these ideas?

I believe a Citizen Legislature should number 450 citizens—about the size of the current House of Representatives—selected at random from the population as a whole rather than geographically, since its members would not officially represent any local constituency. Others have suggested that at least 1,000 members would increase the statistical rigor of representation. But the difference in statistical margin of error between 400 and, say, 1,100 is quite small: (5% at around 400, 4% at around 600, 3% at around 1,100). Considering the added costs, complexity, and difficulty of deliberations involved with such larger groups, I think that 400–500 would be a more manageable size.

Furthermore, I'd suggest that a supermajority vote of 67% for most issues and 75%–80% for certain major issues would address the margin of error issue. A 67% approval vote would mean, at a 5% margin of error, that the Citizen Legislature would have decided the issue with an approval rate of 62%–72%—a sizable majority any way you look at it. The higher the vote required for passage, the more status a decision will rightfully have in the eyes of the public. Perhaps even more important for generating public wisdom, the supermajority requirement also motivates people to craft higher quality—i.e., wiser—legislation that embraces more diverse views and considerations within its conclusions. This goal would be far easier to achieve in this Citizen Legislature than in Congress, thanks to the absence of political gamesmanship because of random selection, term limits (see next paragraph), and a state-of-the-art deliberative process.

The term of office would be three years, with a limit of one term, such that out of 450 members, 150 would be elected each year. This would hinder anyone from making a corruptible career out of their public service, while ensuring that collective knowledge and group culture accumulated among the second- and third-year members to be passed on to newcomers. This, and a month-long training period before new legislators took office, would ameliorate the problems of a chronically novice legislature. Former members of the Citizen Legislature could also serve as advisors and supporters of the current crop of citizen legislators.

Pay would be at current congressional levels ($174,000 in 2011, plus a $20,000 annual pension), and pay raises could only be passed to benefit future citizen legislators, not current ones. Since this pay level is more than three times the median household income in the United States (which is about $50,000)—amounting to about half a million dollars for the three years of service—it would lead most people to eagerly accept their assignment if they were picked. Once they completed their service, they could live off their savings of up to $400,000 or more for many years—if they were reasonably prudent during and after their service—as well as having a pension to look forward to and a remarkable experience to add to their resumé if they chose to seek employment.

Although the power, status, and pay of this job would make most people leap at the chance, I believe this public service should, like jury duty, be mandatory (with some exceptions, as noted below). Selection would be a riveting public spectacle, combining the public attention and energy of elections, lottery winner announcements, and horse and NASCAR races—a political rags-to-riches narrative for most of those selected, covered widely and breathlessly in the press. Every year.

If selectees needed to be excused, they would need to request it, but only for a very limited number of reasons such as serious illness or disability in their immediate family, or having a critical profession such as surgeon or firefighter. One unusual but acceptable reason, as far as I'm concerned, would be that the selectee's normal income is well above the $174,000 citizen legislators would receive. Such wealthy folks would then be replaced by another randomly selected person, biasing the sample in favor of poorer people. After all, the rich person chose not to serve. (Note that a random selection of 450 members would almost always include four to five members of the "top 1 percent," by definition. But that's a far lower number than currently occupies Congress: the average wealth of representatives is over five million dollars; 183 representatives are millionaires; and 33 of them are in the top 1 percent.)

Now let's consider qualifications. I believe there should be none. Think about the qualifications to become a member of Congress today: age, citizenship, residency, and "electability." Although new randomly selected citizen legislators might not be as capable as politicians at handling media, public relations, power dynamics, and fundraising—the skills you need to get yourself elected—all of them would have various forms of intelligence, listening, and thoughtfulness often missing from sound bite– and competition-drenched Washington. Most importantly, they'd be grounded in what it takes to live the life of an ordinary citizen of the United States. Leaders among them would surface quickly and with training, apprenticeship, staff help, and experience, the vast majority of these citizen legislators would become quite competent. By the time they left office, they would be assets out in their communities and often leaders in the nation—sometimes even more so than their politician counterparts.

Not everyone will agree with me about this qualifications issue. So—although I prefer pure random selection (or stratified sampling)—if the issue of qualifications becomes an obstacle, I would propose a special use of random selection to ensure qualified people become citizen legislators. Here's one approach: Convene a randomly selected citizen deliberative council to define the qualifications for being a citizen legislator, avoiding any unduly vague or partisan qualifications. Then have people who wish to be citizen legislators submit applications giving their qualifications and register for the pool of people from which the next crop of citizen legislators will be picked at random. In order to avoid having to verify the qualifications of the thousands of applicants, only the qualifications of *selectees* would be verified. There would be a steep fine for any selectee who was found to have falsified his or her application and he or she would be immediately disqualified, despite having been selected, and a replacement citizen legislator would then be picked at random from the pool. In this way, every citizen legislator would be both randomly selected and qualified to hold the position.

Some people are concerned that many substantive qualifications (such as familiarity with the law) would favor some people (like lawyers) over others. So we could propose that half of the legislators be chosen totally at random (every citizen or voter would be in this pool) and half be chosen from people who meet more stringent qualifications. Part of the job description for membership in the Citizen Legislature could be that the more qualified selectees would help the less qualified people in on-the-job assistance and apprenticeship (regarding skills, not values and issues).

The qualification problem could also be addressed by having good legislative staff to assist the representatives. A pool of experienced, qualified legislative staff members could be established—including top-notch facilitators—from which each new legislator's staff would be randomly selected (to avoid the staff becoming corrupted or entrenched). These staff members would be paid well enough that the minimum three years of service (after which they'd go back into the random pool) would be worth their while, especially with the added status of having worked with the Citizen Legislature.

I believe the Citizen Legislature should replace the House of Representatives. Having both a Citizen Legislature and a House of Representatives feels too close to a duplication of expensive functions. Having legislators selected from the whole country rather than representatives from local districts makes it highly likely that members would come from every state (and if a state is missing, a special selection could pick a person from that state at random), but they wouldn't represent their state in the usual way. They would be working for what's good for the whole country in the context of the world, which is part of their wisdom potential. Their work should be framed that way and defended for the valuable contribution it is. I know this is possibly the most controversial part of this proposal, but I recommend its serious consideration and will continue this chapter on the assumption that it is accepted.

The elected Senate would continue its current roles and rules. It would continue to represent the states and interest groups and it would hold a kind of historical perspective and power-play capacity that the Citizen Legislature, with its rapid turnover, would not be as capable of.

Although the official advisory citizen deliberative panels proposed earlier would not make laws but simply counsel the president and Congress, I believe that a full Citizen Legislature such as I am describing here should, like the House of Representatives, have the power to make and pass laws, not just to recommend or comment on them.

In fact, new laws could and should come from many sources. Legislation could be introduced by the citizen legislators themselves (with the guidance of their experienced staffs). It could be generated using any of the processes described in this book—convened by citizen legislators or anyone else. The People's Voice network could formulate legislation and present it to the Citizen Legislature. A qualifying national initiative, instead of being put to a popular vote (see chapter 11), could be submitted to the Citizen Legislature for deliberation and vote. Advocacy groups could compose legislation and propose it to a citizen legislator who they feel would give them the fairest hearing. That member could submit it to a proposal review panel made up of senior members of the Citizen Legislature (those in their third year as members) to preview and then reject or pass on to an appropriate committee for hearings and framing. (Remember framing? If Deliberapedia is operating, it would be invaluable to the Citizen Legislature.)

With 450 randomly selected citizens in the Citizen Legislature, many deliberations on many issues and bills, using many different processes, could go on simultaneously. The Citizen Legislature could, for example, pick seventy-two of its members at random and hold three simultaneous and independent Citizens Juries (twenty-four people each) about the military budget, a carbon tax, or funding for abortions. The results of these Citizens Juries could be compared and, if they were very similar, legislation could be immediately crafted based on those results. If they were significantly different, the jurors could be mixed together into three new Citizens Juries or Creative Insight Councils to see if there was a convergence. Through such means, more insightfully inclusive—wiser—legislation could be crafted. This would involve only one-sixth of the Citizen Legislature for a couple of weeks and would constitute a more powerful wisdom-generating process than practically anything currently done with public affairs on the planet today.

Random selection could also play other roles in the functioning of the legislature. For example, one-half of the members of each legislative committee (if they decide to have them) could be periodically replaced randomly, so that committees would be less subject to manipulation, while the remaining half of each committee would help ensure that a level of expertise was retained.

If a bill passed the Citizen Legislature with a 67% supermajority—which I believe should be minimum to support its legitimacy and wisdom—it would be sent to the Senate, which would give it priority consideration (e.g., within a month). Approval would be expected unless the Senate could override the Citizen Legislature's vote with its own 67% supermajority. In the other direction, the Citizen Legislature could choose to review any Senate bill (within a month of its passage in the Senate) and override it, if it chose to, with a 67% supermajority. The balance of power would be perfect between the two houses. This would ensure a lot of communication between the two, with political calculations going on, as there are today, to decide when to get together in a resolution committee to work out details of something agreeable to both houses before energy is wasted on legislation that might be overridden by the other house. However, there would be far less horse-trading going on in back rooms, because, although the senators have to deal with interest groups and money pressures in order to get elected, the citizen legislators can't serve another term and aren't beholden to anybody, so they would be inclined to publicize any wheeling and dealing at the expense of the senators responsible. I can even imagine that the Senate might send bills over to the Citizen Legislature as a referendum.

The president, of course, would retain his or her veto power. But his or her veto could be overridden by an average vote of the two houses of 67% (e.g., if the Citizen Legislature voted 75% in favor and the Senate voted 60% in favor, their total would be 135%, which would average out to 67.5% and override the president's veto. And the practice of judicial review remains: The judiciary could rule a law unconstitutional and override it. The Senate and the Citizen Legislature could, of course, change the Constitution, thus overriding the judiciary if necessary, since article 3 of the U.S. Constitution gives the Supreme Court jurisdiction "with such Exceptions and under such Regulations as the Congress shall make"—and the amendment creating the Citizen Legislature would establish it as a branch of Congress.

The moral authority of the Citizen Legislature would be considerable. As time went on, the political consequences of overriding a supermajority decision by the randomly selected Citizen Legislature would grow quite intense.

The days of the broad feeling among the public that their voices are unheard in Washington would also be over. So too would be the widespread despair that the urgent needs of our country and world will never be well addressed. Instead, citizens would begin to feel that there was real hope that major issues and crises would be handled intelligently, even wisely, and that it was truly possible for We the People to set aside petty special interests and get things done.

The era of empowered public wisdom would be born.

CHAPTER 14

Protecting the Power and Integrity of Public Wisdom

Empowered public wisdom is the opposite of the kind of haphazard public ignorance common today that is so readily manipulated by special interests; kept distracted by work, entertainment, and personal struggles; and subdued by conditioned powerlessness and fashionable cynicism.

Empowered public wisdom challenges the status quo. It seeks wherever possible to replace power-over with power-with and power-from-within. It seeks to bring the authority and wisdom of the whole society into the great halls of power and policy. It seeks the capacity to make a difference in the painfully familiar, intractable conditions that degrade our lives and endanger our personal and collective futures.

Empowered public wisdom is exactly what it says: Wise. Public. And Powerful.

Some people won't like that.

Not because they are bad people. They are just trapped in the more privileged roles and narrow worldviews promoted by the stories and systems that are destroying the world. Their spirits are messed with by those stories and systems, virtually as much as the spirits of the more obviously oppressed people's are, albeit in radically different ways. Those who see money, status, and dominance as the field and purpose of the game (or who are lost in their cynicism) are sadly missing the far more fundamental games we play with nature and the human spirit—games we could play so much more productively and with so much more joy. The so-called 1 percent and those manipulated or overwhelmed by them are not the enemy. The stories and systems that trap us all are the challenges we need to face, see clearly, and transform.

Among those who will oppose empowered public wisdom are people with more money than most of us can imagine. The existing system works for them, at least in its shallow, material way. They have the capacity to put well-spun advertisements on primetime television, to pervert journalism, to hire "sock puppet" attackers to trash blogs and online forums, to start astroturf groups that engage activists in their self-serving causes, to write and successfully push through government policies that benefit the wealthy at the expense of the rest of us, to hire infiltrators and surveillance systems to track and undermine the work we do. It is amazing what money can do in today's political environment.

In addition, many traditional activists of all stripes, as well as established political powers like unions, leading pundits, and talk show hosts, may be dubious of citizen deliberative councils because they don't fit the adversarial forms of engagement those players are familiar with. CDCs may seem, at best, to be a dangerous wildcard—unless, of course, the CDC recommends whatever they advocate, or if they think they can get public relations points for participating.

People and groups opposed to CDCs may try to undermine and ridicule our efforts to bring people together, engaging partisans on all sides to say we are promoting dangerous compromises with their enemies. They may say we are messing with America's sacred Constitution, despite the fact that leading architects of that Constitution—particularly Washington, Jefferson, and Madison—all spoke out for the right of the people of each generation to alter it. Jefferson, in fact, insisted that the Constitution should be reworked every nineteen to twenty years! Many people may insist that chaos will result if we use random selection and ordinary people to make policy—despite extensive evidence broadly available that it is precisely this method that could produce the legitimate public wisdom we so desperately need.

Finally, if and where CDCs become established or powerful, there will be concerted efforts to sway them to special-interest conclusions, just as politicians, public agencies, and even trial juries are swayed. The CDC processes themselves must be rigorously transparent and fair; Citizens Juries, in particular, have developed ways to do this. Furthermore, efforts to covertly influence the citizen deliberators with bribery or threats must be prevented and, where it occurs, must be very heavily penalized. High rewards for evidence of such criminal activity would encourage whistleblowers. We should study when and how to make the process public for the sake of transparency and when and how to sequester the delib-erators for security.

We need funds, commitment, and technology to make a political culture based on empowered public wisdom possible in the first place and reliable in its ongoing operation, especially in the face of these challenges. But mostly we need to believe in its importance, recognizing that it will be challenged in direct proportion to its suc-cesses—and we need to be proactive in how we address those challenges.

The first step is to actively look for weaknesses in every-thing we are about to undertake and use powerful creative processes like brainstorming and Dynamic Facilitation to figure out what we can do to counter every effort we can imagine that might corrupt, co-opt, degrade, and suppress our initiatives. We should welcome people who are dubi-ous that we can succeed, invite them into our forums, and help them be specific in naming what we are overlooking and unprepared for—all with the purpose of correcting our oversights and achieving our aims.

Remember that our definition of *wisdom* is "taking into account what needs to be taken into account in order to create broad, long-term benefits." Let us apply that to our own work as rigorously as possible.

Let us do as much development as possible "under the radar"—without broad fanfare—testing and readying our systems and technologies until we are confident that, once released, they will take off rapidly, fueled by popularity and power. Let us be sensitive to timing and responsive to the constantly changing conditions we are already living in. Let us remember the power of high-quality conversation to enable us to be proactively responsive, to be collectively intelligent, to learn our way creatively into a future we don't yet know.

The thoughtful design of collective learning systems—information systems, knowledge systems, conversational systems, networking systems, response and feedback systems—should be a major priority. We want to have and be a fertile, dynamic ecosystem for wise cocreativity that fits our evolving circumstances. We want to increase the ability of the interested public to cocreate the systems that will best serve the broad public. Starting now.

There is no way to foretell what such a systemic design effort will involve in all its specifics. It will necessarily involve much trial and error. Many of these proposals involve advancing the resilience and power of online participatory systems like the People's Voice, Deliberapedia, and the Interactive Voter Choice System. How do we ensure that unique legitimate identities are participating? How do we facilitate crowdsourced evaluation of the truthfulness of information? How do we crowdsource the editing of complex issue information into something the public can easily digest, use, and add their two cents to? How do we make a participatory public policy deliberation and coalition-building forum both sticky (so engaging that it is hard to stop) and viral (so compelling that people quickly share it with their networks)?

Beyond these issues within our movement-building

effort, I see three strategies needed to create a more secure environment for that effort: (a) organize existing citizen deliberators into an advocacy and oversight association, (b) support existing efforts to limit the influence of money in politics, and (c) ensure the integrity of the electoral process.

Organize Citizen Deliberators

From all the evidence I see, the vast majority of people who participate in well-facilitated conversations on public affairs are profoundly and positively affected by the experience. Most of them discover a richer form of citizenship than they have ever known before and are quite excited about that. They feel empowered and that their voices have been heard.

That excitement and empowerment constitute an as-yet-untapped resource for birthing and protecting a culture of high-quality, high-impact dialogue and deliberation. These citizens have sensed a form of citizenship they would love to see practiced more broadly and taken seriously in official decision-making circles. They sense how much it could help their communities and their country.

Their primary concern is that officials or the public will ignore the results of their good work—and this is often the case. Some also have concerns about the quality of the process they have just been through. These concerns are assets. Because these folks are diverse and concerned, but also just ordinary citizens, they are both well motivated and well positioned to promote the use, quality, and influence of organized public conversation on public affairs.

Given that our ability to generate public wisdom is so dependent on the quality of the processes used, how do we ensure that quality? Some people suggest that nonpartisan civic groups, like the League of Women Voters (LWV), and professional facilitator groups, like the National Coalition for Dialogue and Deliberation (NCDD) and the International Association for Public Participation (IAP2), should oversee such processes. But some conservatives question the impartiality of the LWV—and the NCDD and IAP2 could be seen as having a conflict of interest, since their members are in the business of providing professional facilitation to such public conversations. So, although such groups can provide valuable insight and guidance, they simply do not have the moral authority possessed by ordinary citizens to perform this potentially highly charged oversight function. So I propose that these "ordinary people" who happen to know about public process are uniquely qualified to impartially monitor the quality of process and facilitation in official participatory democratic initiatives and institutions. Of course, they could and should ally themselves with and consult with nonpartisan groups and process professionals. But they should retain their independent "people's voice."

This oversight role, though seldom noted, is crucial. Our goal here is the creation of empowered public wisdom. The level of collective wisdom that can be created in a conversation is heavily dependent on the process used and the quality of facilitation. The broad public and public officials are in no way equipped to understand that fact and evaluate how it plays out in any given deliberative activity. So a public engagement event can produce poor results, and quite often observers—from the general public to academic researchers—assume that it is just not possible to get different people to think well together. The energy for promoting empowered public wisdom is seriously undermined by this dynamic.

In short, process and facilitation are not only vital sources of our power but are also potentially our greatest vulnerability. This vulnerability is accentuated by the fact that some of the most commonly used processes and professional facilitators do not have the capacity to generate collective wisdom among diverse ordinary people. When most leaders in the political realm think of public dialogue, deliberation, and participation, they often think of the mainstream processes that won't deliver the kind of empowered public wisdom we need and want. Focused on maximum participation, few in the participatory democracy movement pay much attention to the wisdom of the outcomes or the inclusive legitimacy of the public voice that emerges from public engagement initiatives. This fact is readily used by political players trying to make a show of public engagement while actually restricting the wisdom and power of the public in the process. Furthermore, with truly bad process and facilitation, collective stupidity can be generated that opens the whole idea to ridicule and manipulation.

This is why it is critically important to have principled,

knowledgeable oversight of the processes and facilitation used in our efforts to generate empowered public wisdom. While I am very open to other strategies to achieve this, I have not yet found a more promising approach than organizing ordinary citizens who have previously engaged in public dialogue and deliberation on public issues.

As a first step I would find people who had participated in some of the most empowered and wise processes, who knew something already about the power and public wisdom possible through this kind of activity. We might engage participants in some Citizens Juries that had impact, some members of Oregon's Citizens' Initiative Review, members of Wisdom Councils, some participants in community visioning and revitalization dialogues, and so on. Professional facilitators and conveners in NCDD and IAP2 could point us to successful initiatives, and the participants from those initiatives could be located and engaged.

This group—perhaps called American Citizens Engaged (ACE)—could ultimately include people who had been part of *any* formally convened discussion of public issues—even participants in public hearings and juries that involved public issues—even if they thought the process they had been involved in was horrible and their results ignored. They, too, have energies that could be channeled to promote high-quality empowered public engagements.

However, at the beginning I think it is vital to convene citizens who have experienced the kind of processes that we are most interested in promoting—processes capable of generating empowered public wisdom. Twenty to one hundred of these citizen-founders at the core of ACE, supported by those of us familiar with the ins and outs of the process, could guide it toward performing its highest function of ensuring responsible use of the most effective methods for generating and empowering public wisdom.

Now, that is only the most important of ACE's potential functions. It could have a far broader role as well: catalyzing a dynamic culture of dialogue and deliberation as part of engaging citizens actively in cocreating the long-term well-being of their communities, country, and world.

ACE could provide social networking services to its members and offer them training in dialogic political theory, facilitation, public relations and advocacy work, coalition building, and other skills to support the network's purpose. It could organize them as a force to promote broader use of citizen engagement that is effective, judicious, and empowered. It could educate the philanthropic community about the value of funding high-quality citizen engagement, public participation, and, above all, empowered public wisdom. It could promote studies into factors that influence the use, quality, wisdom, impact, and appreciation of citizen engagement practices and institutions. Its members could be leaders in the People's Voice network. And it could provide guidance to public officials who support public deliberations. If and when a Citizen Legislature is established, ACE could provide the kind of strategic continuity for the citizen legislators that political parties provide for traditional members of Congress.

ACE would liaise closely with NCDD, IAP2, the League

of Women Voters, and other networks of public engagement professionals—especially to recruit new ACE members, but also to better understand how to assess process quality and to evaluate public engagement proposals, processes, initiatives, and institutions. It would work with participation-oriented politicians, public officials, and media to promote understanding of and demand for citizen engagement and empowered public wisdom in governance. It could even work with groups promoting volunteerism, activism, stakeholder conversations, community renewal and resilience, and other public betterment efforts to promote broader, more effective, and integrated citizen engagement in public affairs.

Ultimately ACE would have hundreds of thousands of members, a population that would grow rapidly as more public conversations on public issues were held. It could itself convene and facilitate such conversations, often to showcase what was possible. It would become a major presence in democratic political culture. Most importantly, it would nurture and protect empowered public wisdom so it could grow fully capable of shaping a positive future for life on earth.

Reduce Special-Interest Manipulation of Politics and Elections

While change can happen in many ways and come from many sources, our capacity to make bottom-up institutional changes will almost certainly involve elections. Although it is possible to create political and governmental institutions from scratch, it is more likely that the citizens of the United States will be voting on any significant future changes in America's political and governmental processes. In the early twenty-first century those processes are themselves seriously compromised—and those compromised systems are being used to systematically dismantle what little democracy we have and to corrupt our republic. So while we develop ways to transform democracy into something healthy and wise, we need to support efforts to keep it from dying altogether. Ultimately, we need to be able to vote and have our votes count. The following describes various existing approaches that deserve our support.

Defend democratic rights over corporate rights

Corporations have for centuries found ways (and allies) to expand their alleged rights to take precedent over real democracy and the rights of people, communities, governments, and nature.

There are many emerging strategies to address this problem, and at the time of this writing there is widespread debate among advocates of the different approaches. My own preference would be for these diverse advocates to come together around one integral strategy—a strategy that includes and/or effectively transcends most or all of their different approaches—a united strategy more powerful and wise than anything currently being proposed. If the diverse strategists cannot do this among themselves, perhaps someone could enlist the help of dozens if not hundreds of the most influential activists and organizations whose work is impeded by corporate domination. The advocates of the various strategies could then present their arguments to these powerful political players for deliberation. With help—perhaps with Dynamic Facilitation—these leading activists and organizations could then discover or design a strategic vision they could all agree on, which embraced the values of all the approaches in a synergistic way.

The strategies I currently see are the following:

1. *Community declarations of independence from corporate domination.* This strategy bypasses corporate "personhood" and corporations' claim of constitutional "rights" associated with persons. It also addresses the problem of corporations' legally wielding the Constitution's Commerce Clause to override municipal and state level decisions; legally violating the constitutional rights of citizens and communities at will through their immunity to rights enforcement; and using state and federal preemption to override community self-government. To succeed, this approach requires hundreds or thousands of communities to pass resolutions and successfully resist government intervention and corporate public relations and economic pressure. Ultimately this may prove to be a nonviolent revolutionary approach in the tradition of Gandhi and King, as codified by Harvard's Gene Sharp. Principled noncooperation suggests that "they

can't put us *all* in prison. Our protests will make it increasingly difficult for them to function, especially as more people—including progressive corporate managers, staff, stockholders, and political elites—come see the justice of our cause." While extreme, this approach is seen as necessary by those who feel that all due process avenues of redress are blocked by corporate domination of politics and government. For more on this approach, see www.celdf.org.

2. *A constitutional amendment to declare that corporations are not natural persons.* This would state that corporations don't have the civil rights of persons. A popular option, this may or may not override the Supreme Court's now infamous Citizens United decision, which some suggest was based not on corporate personhood but on the rights of the broad citizenry to hear corporate-sponsored political arguments. Also, since constitutional amendments are notoriously hard to pass, this strategy requires a truly massive organizing effort. However, its success would remove a major pillar of corporate political power in one blow. For more on this approach, see www.movetoamend.org.

3. *A constitutional amendment to require that all campaigns for federal office be financed exclusively with public funds.* This would prohibit expenditures from any other source, including the candidate, and it would prohibit independent support or opposition ads. This may leave loopholes like the use of so-called independent issue ads that promote or attack a candidate's views or char-

acter without mentioning them personally, as well as violations that impact the election but aren't finally punished or invalidated until long after it is over. This strategy also faces the above-mentioned challenges of passing a constitutional amendment. For one version of this approach see www.publiccampaign.org. See also "Campaign finance reform" below.

4. *A congressional declaration that the federal courts, including the Supreme Court, do not have jurisdiction over political matters.* This declaration, as per article 3 of the Constitution, simply reasserts Congress's constitutional right to manage elections. This could, however, trigger a constitutional crisis, which could unfold unpredictably and potentially chaotically. To the extent corporate interests currently control Congress, this approach would only work with truly massive popular support (and, in the worst case scenario, with support from the police and the army). For more on this approach see www.bit.ly/AgGcsn.

5. *Federal laws—and in some cases state laws—that reduce the range of corporate political power without directly tackling the underlying challenge of corporations' rights to dominate the political process.* Below are four ideas I've seen to sidestep the problem of the Supreme Court's decisions. Most have been dropped, but could be picked up again. Although possibly doable in the short run, creative corporate staff—legal, public relations, and strategic planners—will almost certainly find ways to prevail around these.

a. Amend the laws on corporate governance to assure that stockholders explicitly approve political expenditures by the companies they hold shares in.

b. Restrict campaign contributions by government contractors (and sometimes other organizations who have recently received money from the government, such as subsidies and special tax exemptions). Alternatively, when contractors apply for contracts, require them to disclose the contributions they have made to politicians and advocacy groups involved in elections.

c. Prevent campaign contributions from any American corporation controlled by foreign governments.

d. Strengthen conflict-of-interest laws that pertain to government officials to include anything that significantly benefits a corporation. For example, an elected official would not be free to vote on health care policy if pharmaceutical companies and health insurers are major donors to his or her campaign. (Someone even proposed requiring elected officials to wear uniforms like racing car drivers displaying the logos of their corporate sponsors!)

6. *Increased capacity for citizens, communities, and states to generate empowered public wisdom.* This, to the extent it is developed, can create a wise We the People capable of resisting any attempt to control them unjustly or unwisely. As you know, that's what this book is about. But people need to understand this and believe it is possible and worthwhile, so this strategy would likely

be a long process. The longer it took, the more corporate domination could become entrenched.

7. *A reduction of power of giant corporations by building alternative (mostly local and green) economies.* Uncouple livelihood, production, consumption, and all other forms of meeting human needs from the corporate-controlled global economy. This approach will likely gather steam as global economies falter and peak oil and other resource limits undermine the ability of mass economies to satisfy the needs of workers and consumers—e.g., when Walmart can no longer offer low prices because of high transportation costs and unrest in China. To a certain extent, this is inevitable. The transition will be bumpy and/or catastrophic to the extent communities delay their preparations and don't proceed with conscious intention and responsive planning. And as communities try to withdraw from the global economy, certain multinational corporate forces will put obstacles in their way and continue to degrade the larger environment within which those communities struggle. For one of the many websites on this approach, see www.geo.coop/about.

8. *The possibility that corporate domination will die from a million cuts or mosquito bites.* This strategy depends on things like the Occupy movement; YouTube creativity; critiques on blogs; popular movies with anticorporate themes (think Michael Moore and *Wall Street*); anticorporate art, music, and performances; boycotts; stockholder activism; violence and property destruction;

thousands of groups and communities taking this or that political or economic protest action; and so on. All of those would grow into an overwhelming cacophony of populist upheaval as living conditions deteriorate and people have less and less to lose and more desperately want to bring down the "bad guys." This strategy includes the idea that certain corporations and businesses (especially local ones) will do good things and will then use their social responsibility for market advantage, increasing the dynamic tension against the "bad guys." All this creates an energized context for radical change, including voluntary change from within corporations. A major risk of this extremely likely and nonlinear strategy is that as things get worse, fascist and totalitarian tendencies also increase, often on a populist wave.

Campaign finance reform

Although many reforms in this area have been set back by recent Supreme Court decisions, we should continue to support organizations and innovators working in the area, because the legal and political environment could change at any time and private money is public wisdom's primary competitor for influence in America's politics and governance. Here are some of the leading proposals, some of which have many variants:

■ Limit the amount of money that a candidate or party can spend in a campaign.

- Limit the size of donations people and organizations can make to a campaign, and close loopholes that allow them to get around those limits.
- Strengthen political contribution disclosure requirements for both recipients and donors.
- Use public funds to finance *all* campaigns—or to support candidates who refuse large (or all) private and organizational donations (some variants propose public matching funds for the first $100 or $250 of each donation, which increases the value of small donations).
- "Clean Elections." Combine elements of the previous proposals: Candidates qualify for a significant but fixed amount of public funding by gathering a large number of signatures and very small donations, beyond which they do no further fundraising. They can then receive additional funding to match an opponent who is funded by large private donations or to match funds spent by independent political groups who attack them.
- "Voting with Dollars." Provide all citizens with a publicly funded $50 voucher they can distribute to candidates or parties of their choice. Combine this with a system that routes every campaign contribution through the Federal Election Commission, who masks its source, breaks it up, and recombines it with other donations over days, so that by the time it reaches the campaigns it is an anonymous flow of money.

Insure the Integrity of the Voting System

Voting is to mass democracy what air is to an organism. Voting is not the most important thing we need to attend to every day, but in our civic life, serious corruption of the voting process makes the rest kind of pointless. The following proposals address current weaknesses in the integrity of our voting system.

Secure or abolish voting machines

There is compelling evidence that electronic voting machines can be hacked and disturbing evidence that they have been. This is unacceptable and should be investigated with a level of outraged determination that exceeds our investigation into virtually any other crime. If we are going to use electronic voting systems, they must, must, must be secure—and the most brilliant hackers and criminal minds must be recruited to find loopholes that can be corrected. Alan Kay proposes that the voting machine print out for the voter a paper copy of his or her votes, with a confidential and unique number assigned to their ballot. After the election, all votes are publicly listed on the internet with their codes such that anyone can anonymously verify their vote was counted and that all the votes add up to the announced outcome. To avoid electronic ballot stuffing, the number of voters at any polling place can be verified by partisan poll watchers and poll volunteers. If we cannot guarantee the total security of our electronic voting systems, we must return to paper ballots.

Promote the Voter Bill of Rights

There are so many ways to mess with our collective ability to have an impact with our votes, and to realize our Founders' seemingly simple electoral ideal of "one person, one vote." A number of democracy advocacy organizations have come up with a list of reforms to deal with the worst electoral diseases and abuses. These vary slightly among those groups, but I've listed here twelve reforms that cover those variations. The first reform overlaps with my "Secure or abolish voting machines" section above, and the eighth reform overlaps with my "Defend democratic rights over corporate rights" section. You can learn more about any of these by searching the internet for "voter bill of rights" or the specific topic. (Note: Many states have their own "Voters' Bill of Rights." While these are great, they are not what I am referring to here.)

1. Guarantee a voter-verified paper trail for all voting machines (or guarantee a voter-marked paper ballot for all voting).
2. Replace partisan oversight with nonpartisan election commissions.
3. Celebrate democracy: make Election Day a national holiday. (Others recommend a weekend. Neal Gorenflo goes even further: "Elections should be multi-day national holidays. Citizens need substantial time to educate themselves, engage in dialog, make decisions, and elect officials to be truly effective. Why not create weeks-long civic festivals where the focal point is civic

211

processes with accompanying public marches, galas, performances, fairs, and the like?" These would also be ideal times to hold citizen deliberative councils.)

4. Make it easier to vote.
5. Count every vote.
6. Reenfranchise ex-felons and nonfelons.
7. Implement instant runoff voting (IRV) and proportional representation (PR).
8. Replace big-money control with public financing and equal airtime.
9. Guarantee equal access to the ballot and debates (to all parties getting support from at least, say, 10 percent of the voters).
10. Abolish the electoral college.
11. Enact statehood for the District of Columbia.
12. Pass a constitutional amendment confirming the right to vote.

To this list I would add reforming the redistricting process through which the boundaries of electoral districts are redrawn after each census. To prevent gerrymandering—in which legislators adjust districts to help ensure their reelection—the process should be more transparent, less controlled by partisan interests, and centrally involve citizen deliberation—either to do the redistricting or to review and validate its fairness when it is completed.

Conclusion

Empowered public wisdom is the next great evolutionary step for democracy. It will succeed to the extent we promote it wholeheartedly, develop it brilliantly, and protect it vigilantly and tenaciously. It is the greatest creation we could possibly give ourselves and our children's grandchildren—because from it can flow every good thing the world could ever need.

We don't have to know all about what it is. We just have to hunger for it to come to pass among us.

CHAPTER 15

What Role Will *You* Play?

The implications of what is written here are profound. Democracy is capable of far more than we realized—and so are we. The vision in this book is possible—and that possibility challenges us to make it real.

It is time to make wisdom the natural product of democracy in the twenty-first century.

What role will you play?

- Create inspiring videos about this vision . . .
- Help develop websites that empower the People's Voice . . .
- Champion empowered public wisdom through blogs, Twitter, social networks . . .
- Spread the word in schools, activist networks, community groups, churches, temples . . .
- Challenge politicians to sign the Politicians Pledge . . .
- Organize community Wisdom Councils, Open Spaces, World Cafés, study circles . . .
- Fund organizers, conferences, media, and initiatives to get this show on the road in time to make a difference . . .
- Help start a People's Voice political party . . .
- Recruit participants for grassroots deliberations and

Deliberapedia, members for American Citizens Engaged, or volunteers for other aspects of this project...

- Envision new and better ways to do all of this...

Join our community at www.empoweringpublicwisdom .us to share *your* passion and gifts on this extraordinary adventure to remake our communities, our country, and the future of our world.

Appendix 1:
An Annotated List of Powerful Participatory Processes, with Links

There are hundreds of ways to engage citizens and stakeholders creatively in dialogue, deliberation, shared reflections, and action to improve the conditions and capacities of their community. The more than fifty methods described below exemplify approaches that can improve the capacity of a community to generate collective intelligence and wisdom to apply to its own problems and dreams. Methods such as these are the seeds of wiser forms of democracy.

21st Century Town Meetings. AmericaSpeaks organizes large-scale day-long forums engaging thousands of citizens—both face-to-face and through telecommunications links, integrated with laptop computer– and keypad-polling technologies—to deliberate on public issues and provide input to shape government policies. Decision-makers are often included as regular participants. See www.americaspeaks.org.

Appreciative Inquiry. Instead of seeking to solve problems, we can inquire into "the best of the past and present" in our organizations and communities—and then share what we find in ways that "ignite the collective imagination of what might be." See www.appreciative-inquiry.org.

argument mapping. Visual presentation of the arguments and evidence involved in an issue, with arrows showing their connections, can help deliberation tremendously. See www.en.wikipedia.org/wiki/Argument_map.

Asset-Based Community Development (ABCD). Communities can grow stronger by exploring and organizing all the gifts that citizens and associations (formal and informal) can bring to their community life, rather than by treating people as problems and clients. ABCD gathers data about this and makes the connections. See www.co-intelligence.org/P-assetbasedcommdev.html.

Canada's *Maclean's* experiment, "The People's Verdict." A dozen ordinary Canadians selected for their differences, who met under the media spotlight for three days with one of the world's top negotiation specialists, came up with a common vision for the future of their country. This one-time event, organized in 1991 by *Maclean's,* Canada's leading newsweekly, presages the potential for citizen deliberative councils at the national level. See www.co-intelligence.org/S-Canadaadversariesdream.html.

charrette. A hands-on interactive session—often involving subgroup sessions—where professionals and ordinary citizens together generate design solutions to a public issue or architecture/land use problem that integrate the contributions and interests of a variety of stakeholders. See www.en.wikipedia.org/wiki/Charrette.

choice-creating. Not specifically a process, but "the quality of being and thinking that often happens after a crisis, when people drop their roles, express their true feelings, and join with others to creatively seek what's best for all." Often associated with Dynamic Facilitation. See www.tobe.net/CC/choice-creating.html.

citizen consensus councils (CCCs). Diverse citizens are convened to seek, with the help of professional facilitation, shared understandings, solutions, and wisdom about social concerns. Their unanimous conclusions are publicized to their entire community or country. CCCs are citizen deliberative councils that operate by consensus. Examples include Consensus Conferences, Wisdom Councils, and Canada's *Maclean's* experiment. See www.co-intelligence.org/P-citizenCC.html.

citizen councilor forums. Officially registered volunteer citizens agree to gather, when requested by the public official in charge of their forum program, in small study groups in their homes, workplaces, or public gathering spots to study, discuss, and then offer advice to the government and community regarding their assigned issue. See www.kingcounty.gov/operations/auditor/community -forums.aspx.

citizen deliberative councils (CDCs). Temporary, face-to-face councils of a dozen or more citizens whose diversity reflects that of their community, state, or country. Usually council members are selected at random, often with additional criteria to ensure gender, racial, socioeconomic, and other diversity. Convened for two to ten (or, rarely, more) days to consider some public concern, they learn about it (often by hearing and cross-examining diverse experts), reflect on it together (usually with the help of a professional facilitator or moderator), and craft a collective statement, which they then announce to the public and/or relevant officials and agencies (often through a press conference), after which they disband. Examples include Citizens Juries, Consensus Conferences, Planning Cells, the Canadian *Maclean's* experiment, Wisdom Councils, and Creative Insight Councils. (See also citizen reflective councils.) See co-intelligence.org/P-CDCs.html and Tom Atlee's *The Tao of Democracy: Using Co-Intelligence to Create a World that Works for All*—www.taoofdemocracy.org.

citizen panels. A popular name for citizen deliberative councils, as explored by John Gastil in his book *By Popular Demand*, which describes five ways to use them to establish real answerability in electoral politics and the legislative process.

citizen reflective councils. Another name for varieties of citizen deliberative council that tend to be more open-ended, emotional, and creative than the word "deliberation" often implies. "Reflective" suggests both that they are reflecting about their community and that their members reflect (rather than politically represent) the diverse members of their community. See www.co-intelligence.org/P-CRC.html.

Citizens' Assembly. An officially convened panel consisting of a man and a woman randomly selected from each legislative district—usually numbering one hundred or more—who meet every other weekend for months to study, take public testimony, deliberate, and make recommendations on an issue too full of controversy or conflict

of interest to be handled well by the legislature. See www
.coop-tools.ca/mini_public.

Citizens Juries. The most basic and widely practiced
citizen deliberative council, with twelve to twenty-four
participants. Pioneered in the United States. See www
.jefferson-center.org/citizens_jury.htm and Ned Crosby's
*Healthy Democracy: Empowering a Clear and Informed Voice of
the People.* See also citizen panels.

civic journalism. Civic journalism attempts to engage
people in public life by finding out what they are concerned about, providing them with balanced information about the issues involved, getting them talking about
those issues, and reflecting what they say back to the
larger community in broadcast, print, and online media.
See www.pewcenter.org/doingcj/speeches/index.html.

Community-Based Watershed Management Councils.
Stakeholders from public, private, and nonprofit sectors come together regularly to care for the watershed
resources they all depend on. See mckenziewc.org/about
.htm for an example and www.umich.edu/~crpgroup/sites
.html for national resources.

community quality of life indicators. Communities
around the world have developed local statistics to measure their collective well-being, providing them with feedback about how they're doing. See www.co-intelligence
.org/P-qualtylifeindicators.html.

Commons Cafés. Ten people are selected from four
very diverse groups (e.g., an inner-city church, a golf club)
and convened such that one person from each group is at

each of ten four-person tables. Each table has cards with questions about one's life, which the participants answer, sharing their lives with each other. Designed to humanize the Other, across boundaries. See www.commonway.org.

community vision programs. See scenario and visioning work, below.

Consensus Conferences. Citizen deliberative councils that are much like Citizens Juries except (a) panelists participate more in selecting experts to testify before them, (b) expert testimony is taken in a public forum, and (c) a panel's final product is a consensus statement. A rare example of citizen deliberative council being institutionalized as a part of government—in Denmark, where it was pioneered to advise Parliament on controversial technical issues. See www.co-intelligence.org/P-DanishTechPanels.html.

Consensus Councils. These bring together the full diversity of stakeholders around a contentious issue to agree on recommendations to policy-makers. These have existed for several years in Montana and North Dakota, but a United States Consensus Council has recently been established. See www.agree.org/what.

consensus process. A broad category of processes that endeavor to weave the actual diversity of the participants into understandings and solutions that make sense for all those involved, notably characterized by substantively addressing the concerns of participants. See www.co -intelligence.org/P-consensus.html.

Conversation Cafés. Small, lightly facilitated gatherings held regularly in a specific public place, usually an actual café, and open to the public. They usually start and end with a go-round much like a listening circle, with the body of the conversation being open dialogue. Normally convened around a topic. Often a city or town will have many Conversation Cafés people can attend. See www .conversationcafe.org.

Creative Insight Council (CIC). A promising experimental process in which a diverse microcosm of a community—joined by experts, stakeholders, and/or partisans as participating witnesses—explore a predefined issue in a dynamically facilitated choice-creating conversation designed to generate breakthrough solutions. See www .tobe.net/DF/DF/page52/page52.html.

deliberation, public. This means that citizens are considering an issue carefully, hearing many sides, and considering various possible outcomes and trade-offs, in an effort to come to useful public judgment about how the issue should be addressed. This is the core of deliberative democracy. See www.co-intelligence.org/deliberation.html.

Deliberative Polling. Hundreds of citizens are surveyed about an issue and then study it and deliberate about it. They are then polled again. Repeated demonstrations of this process have shown that people's views on an issue change when they have a chance to learn and think about all sides of it. See www.cdd.stanford.edu/polls /docs/summary.

dialogue. Increasingly this term is used to describe conversation in which participants all feel heard, which enables them to actually learn and/or accomplish things together. Another definition: Shared exploration toward greater understanding, relationship, and/or possibility. See www.co-intelligence.org/P-dialogue.html, which, among other things, provides a useful list comparing dialogue and debate.

dialogue, Bohmian. A form of dialogue in which participants attend to the assumptions behind their own and each other's responses and thoughts. This approach, founded by quantum physicist David Bohm and spiritual teacher Jiddu Krishnamurti, often shifts conversation from an exchange of ideas to a shared flow of meaning. See www.david-bohm.net/dialogue.

Dynamic Facilitation (DF). An open-ended and highly creative process grounded in the power of helping people feel truly heard and following where their interest and energy take them, rather than following a preestablished agenda. It helps groups wrestle creatively with difficult problems such that they often stumble into truly innovative insights and solutions. DF includes a potent reframing of *conflicts* as *concerns*. It is most powerfully applied to community, state, or national affairs in the form of Wisdom Councils. See www.co-intelligence.org /P-dynamicfacilitation.html and www.tobe.net.

fishbowl. A small group of people (usually four to eight) sit in a circle discussing a specific topic in full view of a larger group of interested listeners, who sit in a circle around them. Widely useful with many variations. Described at www.kstoolkit.org/Fish+Bowl.

framing for deliberation. A fair presentation of the

range of popular approaches—usually three to five—to address an issue, along with the arguments and evidence associated with each one, to give deliberators a neutral starting point for their deliberations. See www.public -agenda .org/files/pdf/Reframing%20Framing_0.pdf.

Future Search. Representative stakeholders are gathered together to review or cocreate the future of their organization, community, or situation. They look at their shared history, the forces currently shaping their shared lives, and the visions they can all buy into—and then they self-organize into ongoing action groups to further the vision(s) they created together. See www.co-intelligence .org/P-futuresearch.html.

general assembly. A grassroots consensus decision-making process used by hundreds or thousands of people involved in a workplace, neighborhood, or activist group usually using hand signals to indicate support, concerns, process issues, etc. Made recently famous by the Occupy movement. See www.harpers.org/archive/2011/10/hbc -90008270.

Holistic Management. This draws together all the important people and resources relating to an issue to generate clarifying holistic statements of their desired quality of life. It involves taking time to check all future decisions against that statement. See www.co-intelligence. org/P-holisticmgmt.html.

intergroup dialogue. People from different social identity groups gather for a series of meetings designed to help participants gain a deeper understanding of diversity and

justice issues. See www.igr.umich.edu/documents
/Intergroup%20Dialogue%20Overview.pdf.

listening circle. A group of three to thirty (and some-times more) people sit in a circle and take turns "speaking from the heart." Usually the speaker holds an object (a "talking stick," a stone, even a stapler) and, when done speaking, passes the object to the person on their left, who may then speak. There is no cross talk or interruptions. If a number of rounds are done, the dialogue tends to deepen. Common variations and alternate names include talking circle, PeerSpirit circle, council circle and circle process. See www.co-intelligence.org/P-listeningcircles.html.

Listening Project. Trained interviewers canvass a com-munity with questions designed to engage people with community or national issues. The role of the interviewers is to listen well. People change during the interviews, often getting involved in addressing the issues they discussed. See www.co-intelligence.org/P-listeningpjts.html.

multiple-viewpoint drama. What does a public issue look like when you see all sides in their raw, dramatic expression? Anna Deavere Smith created two monologue docudramas acting out the actual statements of people she interviewed, people who were associated with riots in Los Angeles and New York City. The Laramie Project did a similar work around a gay hate crime. Such dramas could be used to make the human complexity of any issue more real to decision-makers and citizens in their deliberations. See www.co-intelligence.org/S-multipleviewptdrama.html.

Natural Resource Leadership Institutes. Diverse stakeholders from all sectors—many of them long-time opponents gridlocked over natural resource conflicts—come together for six three-day sessions to explore how to creatively resolve such conflicts in their state. Their learning and their actions often bring about a shift. See www.ncsu.edu/nrli.

neighborhood councils. A number of cities have provided a means for neighborhoods to organize themselves, to receive official recognition, and to provide themselves with a forum for deliberating about their neighborhood issues and maintaining relationships with other neighborhoods and with city officials and agencies. See lacityneighborhoods.com for an example. These are also sometimes called neighborhood assemblies (sfnan.org)—and much excitement has been generated recently about the neighborhood assemblies spontaneously formed in Argentina in response to their economic crises. See www.commondreams.org/headlines02/0325-06.htm.

Nonviolent Communication. A process through which one person can empathize with the needs underlying another's reactions and seek ways those needs can be served that satisfy everyone involved. It can be done in group settings, but even that usually involves working one-on-one. See www.co-intelligence.org/P-nonviolentcomm.html.

Open Forums. Arny Mindell believes that the solutions to our conflicts and problems lie in the heart of the disturbances we try so hard to avoid, and that we can find those solutions through a process that encourages all the voices involved to speak to each other, and be heard. See www.democracyinnovations.org/openforums.html and Mindell's *The Deep Democracy of Open Forums.*

Open Space Technology. An amazingly simple way for dozens or hundreds of people to get together and talk about a topic they're all passionately interested in—and have it feel more like a coffee break than a conference. There is no agenda other than the diverse workshops and conversations that the participants create together at the beginning and then attend and modify as the conference continues. See www.co-intelligence.org/P-Openspace.html.

Participatory Budgeting. In Porto Alegre, Brazil (and more than one hundred other cities), thousands of citizens and NGOs (nongovernmental organizations) participate every year in deciding how their municipal budget will be spent—and then oversee the resulting public works projects. Deliberations are organized both by neighborhood and by topic (education, transportation, etc.). See www.participatorybudgeting.org.

Planning Cells. Numerous, simultaneous, twenty-five-person citizen deliberative councils (cells) all address the same subject. Participants spend much of their time in five-person subgroups. The cells' diverse final statements are integrated into one "Citizens' Report." Pioneered in Germany. See www.planet-thanet.fsnet.co.uk/groups/wdd /99_planning_cells.htm.

Positive Deviance. This practice helps communities become aware of—and spread—successful solutions to shared problems that are being practiced by certain

unrecognized community members. See
www.positivedeviance.org.

Principled Negotiation. Roger Fisher's and William
Ury's classic 1981 *Getting to Yes* suggests resolving conflicts
by (1) separating the people from the problem; (2) focus-
ing on interests, not positions; (3) inventing options for
mutual gain; and (4) insisting on objective criteria. See
colorado.edu/conflict/peace/treatment/pricneg.htm.

Public Conversation Project. Pro-life and pro-choice
activists shared their stories, beliefs, and concerns in non-
polarized dialogues, sponsored by some family systems
therapists, and achieved remarkable mutual understandings. The method has since been used with polarized
environmental stakeholders and other groups. See www
.publicconversations.org.

Reuniting America. A program to help local citizens
join in bridge-building conversations about democracy
and civic concerns using simple powerful guidelines for
hosts and participants. See www.reunitingamerica.org.

scenario and visioning work. A broad category of methods for creating shared visions or carefully considering different possible futures. Evidence suggests that looking into
the future is one of the healthiest, most powerful things
any group or community can do. See www.co-intelligence
.org/P-scenario-visioning.html.

Search for Common Ground. This process uses personal stories, reflective/active listening, genuine curiosity/
real questioning, and searching for points of authentic
connection and resonance between one's own experience,

values, and ideas and those of one's adversaries. It helps adversaries focus on truly hearing each other and discovering problems and aspirations that both sides care about and can address together with shared action. See www.sfcg .org/programmes/us/us_life.html.

salons. Informal, often regular gatherings of friends (or people in someone's network) for high-quality conversation about things they care about, often over food and drink, or tea or coffee, often in someone's home. See *The Joy of Conversation: The Complete Guide to Salons* by Jaida n'ha Sandra and the editors of *Utne* magazine.

study circles. Ordinary people get together once or twice a week to study public issues together, explore what they think should be done about them, and, often, take action together. Study circles are often woven into broadly inclusive community programs around issues like race, police relations, and so on, which sponsor dozens or hundreds of simultaneous study circles and bring together all participants at the conclusion of the program. See www .everyday-democracy.org.

Wisdom Council. A citizen reflective council using Dynamic Facilitation to explore what a randomly selected group of citizens feels is important to them and the community or country where they live and to issue a consensus statement about what they decide. A new Wisdom Council with newly selected members is held—ideally with great fanfare—every three to twelve months in that community or country. This ongoing process is designed to build a strong collective sense of We the

People. See www.co-intelligence.org/P-wisdomcouncil
.html, www.wisedemocracy.org, and Jim Rough's *Society's
Breakthrough! Releasing Essential Wisdom and Virtue in All
the People.*

The World Café. Dozens or hundreds of people show
up for a conversation about a topic that matters to them.
They sit around separate tables (four to five to a table)
and, after twenty to forty minutes of talking, they move to
different tables to continue the conversation. After a few
rounds of this, a lot of interesting ideas will have arisen
and moved around the room. Highlights can be harvested
in a final session all together. See www.theworldcafe.com.

Appendix 2:
Some Areas for Research and Development

We need research that continually improves our ability to generate a coherent, informed, inclusive, trustworthy, legitimate, and wise voice of the whole society. Various deliberative methodologies (and various partisan groups) claim to provide or speak with the legitimate voice of the people. Such claims are often dubious, sometimes inspiring, but never verified with anything remotely as rigorous as the research that demonstrates the efficacy of scientific polling—that is, if you survey a thousand people with a particular survey approach, then you will get the same results (within a small margin of error) if you survey a different thousand people with the same approach. To truly transform politics, we need to establish how to generate a deliberative, coherent, and demonstrably legitimate voice of the whole society.

Serious research on the subject would require courageous, determined, possibility-oriented efforts and considerable funding. Below are five possible areas of research into "empowered public wisdom." They cover information, legitimacy, expense, wisdom, and public engagement.

Information

Rigorous methods have been developed to provide citizen deliberators with balanced briefing materials. These include making sure that three to five competing perspectives are fairly presented—a process often overseen by a mixed-partisan advisory council. However, no briefing can ever be complete, and additional checks on bias are desirable. One intriguing possibility is that after one round of briefings and expert interviews, deliberators split up into research teams to search the web for information and alternative solutions beyond their briefing materials, and compare the results. They could then call on old or new experts to answer questions about what they found. *What would be the costs, benefits, and shortcomings of such a process? Are there better procedures for bringing information into a deliberation beyond what's provided by prepared briefing materials and expert witnesses?*

Legitimacy

Check the similarities and differences among multiple independent CDCs. Random selection, balanced briefing materials, and high-quality group process give CDCs good claim to being a fair voice of a whole society or community. However, little research has been done to see if comparable CDCs come up with comparable results. For example, three Citizens Juries could be convened simultaneously and separately on the same issue. If they came up with fairly similar results (as has been demonstrated with research on public opinion polls), their claim to full legitimacy would have more weight. If they came up with different outcomes, experiments could test new designs, searching for ways to generate reliably similar outcomes without manipulating the content of the conversations. *How can we find and demonstrate a way to produce a legitimate deliberative voice of a whole community or society?*

Check public agreement with CDCs. Survey the recommendations of citizen deliberations on equal footing with mainstream proposals regarding the same issue, to measure the level of agreement between the public and the CDC. If the deliberative recommendations prove unpopular with the public, focus group research could clarify what caused the discrepancy, and experiments could be designed to narrow that discrepancy, possibly including public engagement modes described below.

Expand "the whole" from just citizens to include stakeholders. Stakeholders are people with interests, information, functions, or power related to an issue. Most issues involve some persistent conflict among stakeholders with competing interests. A leading approach to dealing with issues is to convene a full range of stakeholders in problem-solving or conflict-resolution conversations to find solutions that satisfy them all. Though this approach is radically different from citizen deliberative councils (which usually involve stakeholders only as witnesses), it is a fully valid way of cutting the pie of "those concerned" or "the whole community"—as long as it includes "ordinary citizens" among the identified stakeholders in public issues. Obviously wisdom and legitimacy may both be served by doing both citizen- and stakeholder-based deliberations. Some research is needed to learn about the similarities and differences between the results of these two approaches. One research approach would be to convene three Citizens Juries—as envisioned above—and three stakeholder dialogues (using the same stakeholder process), all on the same subject, but independently. Compare the results for similarities, differences, and other lessons. If the results are quite different, mix and match the participants into three to six new independent groups, each of which has a few members from all the previous groups—and then see if *they* come up with comparable results. The Creative Insight Council process may be ideal for this final step.

Expense

Most CDCs cost tens of thousands of dollars to complete. This is small compared to the savings that would often be possible through implementing their broadly supported, sensible policy recommendations, especially on budgetary matters. But it is an obstacle to their rapid acceptance and use. Research could be done to see if 80 percent cost savings could be achieved with no more than a 20 percent reduction in quality—for example, by using

- volunteer pools from which deliberators could be randomly and/or demographically selected;
- asynchronous online deliberations;
- sophisticated conference technologies (like Maestro and videoconferencing);
- crowdsourced briefing materials, e.g., a Deliberapedia

wiki where opposing issue advocates together frame their shared issue for deliberation (see chapter 12); and

■ online interviewing of experts via videoconferencing or even email.

Another approach might be to use a gradient of increasingly expensive methods—opinion polling, Deliberative Polling, online deliberations, and face-to-face CDCs—and use the cheaper methods for less important issues, saving the more expensive approaches for the most important issues (as proposed by international pollster Steven Kull). This approach would benefit from research comparing the policy recommendations resulting from all four approaches on the same issue, to see how well they can substitute for each other. *How can we reduce the costs of citizen deliberation with minimal loss of quality using the internet? Can the development of more accessible participatory forms of quality citizen deliberation enable grassroots, self-organized capacity for collective intelligence in the political sphere?*

Cognitive Capacities

Not only are there diverse kinds of intelligence, but different people are differently endowed with each kind. Cognitive differences and limitations can undermine or enhance productive deliberation. *What has been found that deals well with this, transmuting these differences into cocreative gifts? What other developments are possible to enhance this capacity?*

Wisdom

Wisdom can be defined as insight that takes into account what needs to be taken into account for long-term, broadly beneficial outcomes. Chapter 4 describes multiple sources for public wisdom. Some sources involve simply the humanity and diversity of the deliberators in quality conversations. Ordinary citizens bring common-sense perspectives arising from their community values and their daily lives and aspirations. But their limited information and parochial perspectives may constrain the wisdom they can generate together. So we need to seek other sources: outside experts, materials, or processes which can provide deliberators with broader information and perspective. Experts can enlighten deliberators about the social, spiritual, moral, and scientific aspects of an issue. However, they can also bias, overwhelm, or mystify ordinary citizens. We need elegant combinations of these sources of wisdom to produce "public wisdom" to guide public policy and serve our communities well. *How can we enhance the wisdom of CDCs by including not only issue experts but religious leaders, ethics experts, systems thinkers, and other specialists, materials, or exercises that introduce big-picture, long-term considerations—especially without raising church-state issues, introducing unreasonable bias, or requiring lengthy lessons in abstract concepts?*

Public Engagement

Even if a group of dozens of randomly selected citizens develop wise policies, the public may not understand how that citizen council came up with those recommendations, resulting in lack of public support for their "public wisdom." Furthermore, the public may have useful information, insight, or solutions that could inform a CDC. *How can we engage broader public involvement before, during, and after a CDC, such that the public contributes to, understands, agrees with, and benefits from the public wisdom generated by the CDC?*

Possible approaches include

- online forums where citizens can present, rate, and deliberate on policy options;
- real-time engagement between CDC members and members of the public through chats, instant messaging, conference calls, etc.;
- public hearings and channels for submitting white papers to the CDC;
- online and phone voting on emerging CDC recommendations;
- in-person public dialogues like World Cafés and Conversation Cafés in which all citizens are invited to discuss the issues and CDC recommendations;
- in-person activities like Open Space conferences and study circles that engage the community in learning about and acting on the results of the CDC;

- thorough media reporting on the participants, conversations, and outcomes of citizen councils, allowing vicarious public experience of the deliberative process; and
- large one-day media events involving thousands of people in deliberations that include the results of the CDC. (Although such mega-events can seldom match the deliberative quality of multiday events involving a few dozen randomly selected participants, they can powerfully serve the need for public engagement.)

Suggested Reading

Titles marked with an asterisk * are particularly important for this work.

Baldwin, Christina. *Calling the Circle: The First and Future Culture.* New York: Bantam, 1998.

Briggs, John, and F. David Peat. *Seven Life Lessons of Chaos: Timeless Wisdom from the Science of Change.* New York: Harper-Collins, 1999.

Briskin, Alan, Sheryl Erickson, John Ott, and Tom Callanan. *The Power of Collective Wisdom and the Trap of Collective Folly.* San Francisco: Berrett-Koehler, 2009.

*Brown, Juanita, with David Isaacs and the World Café Community. *The World Café: Shaping Our Futures Through Conversations That Matter.* San Francisco: Berrett-Koehler, 2005.

*Callenbach, Ernest, and Michael Phillips. *A Citizen Legislature.* Berkeley, CA: Banyan Tree Books; Bodega, CA: Clear Glass, 1985.

Capra, Fritjof. *The Web of Life: A New Scientific Understanding of Living Systems.* New York: Anchor Books, 1996.

*Chickering, A. Lawrence, and James S. Turner. *Voice of the People: The Transpartisan Imperative in American Life.* Goleta, CA: da Vinci Press, 2008.

*Crosby, Ned. *Healthy Democracy: Empowering a Clear and Informed Voice of the People.* Edina, MN: Beaver's Pond Press, 2003.

Dahl, Robert A. *Democracy and Its Critics.* New Haven, CT: Yale University Press, 1989.

Dowd, Michael. *Thank God for Evolution: How the Marriage of Science and Religion Will Transform Your Life and Our World.* New York: Viking, 2008.

Ellinor, Linda, and Glenna Gerard. *Dialogue: Rediscovering the*

Transforming Power of Conversation. New York: J. Wiley and Sons, 1998.

*Fisher, Roger, and William Ury. *Getting to Yes: Negotiating Agreement without Giving In.* New York: Penguin, 1981.

*Fishkin, James S. *When the People Speak: Deliberative Democracy and Public Consultation.* New York: Oxford University Press, 2009.

Follett, Mary Parker. *The New State: Group Organization and the Solution of Popular Government.* Whitefish, MT: Kessinger, 2009.

*Gastil, John. *By Popular Demand: Revitalizing Representative Democracy through Deliberative Elections.* Berkeley: University of California Press, 2000.

*Gastil, John, and Peter Levine (eds). *The Deliberative Democracy Handbook: Strategies for Effective Civic Engagement in the 21st Century.* San Francisco: Jossey-Bass, 2005.

Hawken, Paul. *Blessed Unrest: How the Largest Social Movement in History Is Restoring Grace, Justice, and Beauty to the World.* New York: Penguin, 2007.

Hindman, Matthew. *The Myth of Digital Democracy.* Princeton, NJ: Princeton University Press, 2008.

*Holman, Peggy, Tom Devane, and Steven Cady. *The Change Handbook: The Definitive Resource on Today's Best Methods for Engaging Whole Systems.* San Francisco: Berrett-Koehler, 2007.

*Holman, Peggy. *Engaging Emergence: Turning Upheaval into Opportunity.* San Francisco: Berrett-Koehler, 2010.

*Hopkins, Rob. *The Transition Companion: Making Your Community More Resilient in Uncertain Times.* White River Junction, VT: Chelsea Green, 2011.

Johnston, Charles M. *The Creative Imperative: Human Growth and Planetary Evolution.* Berkeley, CA: Celestial Arts, 1984.

Kaner, Sam, Lenny Lind, Catherine Toldi, Sarah Fisk, and Duane Berger. *Facilitator's Guide to Participatory Decision-Making.* Philadelphia: New Society, 1996.

Kretzmann, John P., and John L. McKnight. *Building Communities from the Inside Out: A Path Toward Finding and Mobilizing a Community's Assets.* Evanston, IL: The Asset-Based Community Development Institute, Institute for Policy Research, Northwestern University, 1993.

Lappé, Frances Moore, and Paul Du Bois. *The Quickening of America: Rebuilding Our Nation, Remaking Our Lives.* San Francisco: Jossey-Bass, 1994.

*Lappé, Frances Moore. *Ecomind: Changing the Way We Think, to Create the World We Want.* New York: Nation Books, 2011.

*Leib, Ethan J. *Deliberative Democracy in America: A Proposal for a Popular Branch of Government.* University Park, PA: Pennsylvania State University Press, 2004.

Leighninger, Matt. *The Next Form of Democracy: How Expert Rule Is Giving Way to Shared Governance—and Why Politics Will Never Be the Same.* Nashville, TN: Vanderbilt University Press, 2006.

Lo, Alpha, and Alden Bevington (eds.). *The Open Collaboration Encyclopedia: The Essential Guidebook to Participatory Culture (Version 2.3).* Ross, CA: Pioneer Imprints, 2010.

*McCormick, Joseph, and Steve Bhaerman. *Reuniting America: A Toolkit for Changing the Political Game.* www.reunitingamerica.org, 2011.

Mindell, Arnold. *The Leader as Martial Artist: An Introduction to Deep Democracy.* San Francisco: HarperSanFrancisco, 1992.

Noveck, Beth Simone. *Wiki Government: How Technology Can Make Government Better, Democracy Stronger, and Citizens More Powerful.* Washington, DC: Brookings Institution Press, 2009.

*Oliver, Leonard P. *Study Circles: Coming Together for Personal Growth and Social Change.* Cabin John, MD: Seven Locks Press, 1987.

Ornstein, Robert E., and Paul R. Ehrlich. *New World, New Mind: Moving toward Conscious Evolution.* New York: Simon and Schuster, Touchstone, 1989.

*Owen, Harrison. *Open Space Technology: A User's Guide.* San Francisco: Berrett-Koehler, 1997.

Peavey, Fran. *Heart Politics.* Philadelphia: New Society, 1986.

Rosenberg, Marshall B. *Nonviolent Communication: A Language of Compassion.* Del Mar, CA: PuddleDancer Press, 1999.

*Rough, Jim. *Society's Breakthrough! Releasing Essential Wisdom and Virtue in All the People.* Bloomington, IN: 1st Books Library, 2002.

Sandra, Jaida N'ha. *The Joy of Conversation: The Complete Guide to Salons.* Minneapolis, MN: Utne Reader Books, 1997.

Schneider, Don. *Communicating across the Divides in Our Everyday Lives: A Psychological Field Manual for Constructive Dialogue about Social and Environmental Concerns and the Progress of Civilization.* Eugene, OR: Elkdream Media, 2009.

*Sclove, Richard. *Democracy and Technology.* New York: Guilford Press, 1995.

Shirky, Clay. *Here Comes Everybody: The Power of Organizing without Organizations.* New York: Penguin, 2008.

Sunstein, Cass R. *Infotopia: How Many Minds Produce Knowledge.* New York: Oxford University Press, 2006.

*Taher, Nasreen, ed. *Collective Intelligence: An Introduction.* Hyderabad, India: ICFAI University Press, 2005.

*Tovey, Mark (ed.). *Collective Intelligence: Creating a Prosperous World at Peace.* Oakton, VA: Earth Intelligence Network, 2008.

Waldrop, M. Mitchell. *Complexity: The Emerging Science at the Edge of Order and Chaos.* New York: Simon and Schuster, 1992.

Weisbord, Marvin, and Sandra Janoff. *Future Search: An Action Guide to Finding Common Ground in Organizations and Communities.* San Francisco: Berrett-Koehler, 1995.

Wheatley, Margaret. *Leadership and the New Science: Discovering Order in a Chaotic World.* San Francisco: Berrett-Koehler, 1999.

Wheatley, Margaret, and Deborah Frieze. *Walk Out Walk On: A Learning Journey into Communities Daring to Live the Future Now.* San Francisco: Berrett-Koehler, 2011.

Index

Index

Index

About the Author

TOM ATLEE is the founder of the nonprofit Co-Intelligence Institute, author of *The Tao of Democracy* and *Reflections on Evolutionary Activism,* and lead contributor to *Collective Intelligence: An Introduction* (edited by Nasreen Taher). He has published many articles in alternative journals, collaborated on numerous projects and books, been on several nonprofit boards, and occasionally consulted internationally.

Born in 1947, Atlee was raised as a Quaker peace and social justice activist. On the 1986 Great Peace March, a nine-month trek undertaken by four hundred ordinary people, he experienced bottom-up self-organization and palpable collective intelligence for the first time. This watershed experience changed his life into a search for how to evoke these collective capacities in activist groups, communities, and whole societies. Starting in the mid-1990s, his activist instincts led him to apply his discoveries to the creation of wiser forms of democracy and governance. In 2005 he began a study of evolutionary dynamics that could be used to transform social systems. He is currently exploring the emerging and evolving landscape of green, local, humane, self-organizing, co-intelligent economic innovations—an abundance of vital alternatives he hopes to weave into his next book.

Tom lives simply in a nine-bedroom, consensus-based co-op house in Eugene, Oregon, with a changing population of friends, dogs, cats, chickens, plants, books, and chores. While he spends most of his time glued to his computer, talking passionately with colleagues, or hanging out with his beloved partner, Dulcy Lee, he also enjoys reading, walking, writing poetry, playing twelve-string guitar, watching movies, and learning how to split wood. His daughter, Jennifer Atlee, is a green building professional in New England who loves hiking and can usually think rings around her father. Atlee can be reached by email at cii@igc.org.